Is It Time?

Is It Time?

**Helping Laity and Clergy
Discuss Homosexuality
One Question at a Time**

Adolf Hansen

Abingdon Press
Nashville

IS IT TIME?
HELPING LAITY AND CLERGY DISCUSS HOMOSEXUALITY
ONE QUESTION AT A TIME

Copyright © 2017 by Abingdon Press

ISBN 9781501859731 print

ISBN 9781501859748 epub

17 18 19 20 21 22 23 24 25 26—10 9 8 7 6 5 4 3 2 1

Manufactured in the United States of America

TO

*laity and clergy of The United Methodist Church
at every point on the theological spectrum,
that they may listen to each other,
learn from each other,
and follow the leading of the Holy Spirit
on matters pertaining to homosexuality*

Contents

PART ONE—PHYSICAL AND PSYCHOLOGICAL

Is it time to stop . . .

PART TWO—BIBLICAL AND THEOLOGICAL

Is it time to stop ...

PART THREE—RELATIONAL AND PRACTICAL

Is it time to stop ...

POSTSCRIPT

Is it time to start . . .

Preface

It may not be an exaggeration to say that millions of United Methodists yearn for a time when the fullness of the gospel of Jesus Christ and its transforming power—in the lives of individuals and in the structures of society—can take center stage. For too long we have been engrossed with selected dimensions of the gospel—particularly homosexuality and its effect on human lives—to the exclusion of others.

The question—"Is It Time?"—identifies the overall question of this book. The subtitle—"Helping Laity and Clergy Discuss Homosexuality One Question at a Time"—provides a description of audience, subject, and process. Although the primary audience of this book is the laity and clergy of The United Methodist Church, it can easily be adapted and used with other ecclesiastical judicatories and organizations that resonate with questions raised in some or all of the chapters.

The resources used in writing this book come not only from the academic training and personal experiences of the author but also from the conceptual formulations and existential narratives of hundreds of other people who generously shared their ideas and told me their stories—in writings, videos, and most effectively in personal conversations. Some of these individuals were straight, and some were lesbian, gay, bisexual, transgendered, queer, or questioning. To them I pay tribute and express my deep gratitude.

Colleagues from various contexts read a part or all of the manuscript and provided challenging as well as supportive commentary. I am profoundly appreciative of their input. They are too numerous to identify, but two of them deserve highest praise. First, Naomi Metzger Hansen, an incredibly gifted, caring, and generous individual with whom I have been married for fifty-eight years. She worked with me throughout the process and assisted me not only with typing and proofreading but also in the ongoing discussion of the issues in each chapter. And second, Holly Miller, a renowned author, professor, and editor, who read the entire draft and offered numerous suggestions for communicating more effectively what I was trying to say.

On a personal note, I want to express my heartfelt desire to you, the reader—whether you agree or disagree with what I have written—that you will *pause to reflect* on what I have expressed. I hope you will find those times of reflection helpful to you and useful in your conversations with others—particularly those with whom you disagree.

And, most important to me, my profound yearning is that God will be honored and glorified through this book and will find ways to speak through it when it coincides with what God wants to say.

Introduction

Many books have been written on the subject of homosexuality. So, it's natural to ask: Do we need another?

Most of those books either defend or attack a certain point of view. A limited number of them attempt to bring differing perspectives together. But none that I have located use a Socratic approach—asking questions rather than formulating answers—in dealing with the central issues involved in a discussion of homosexuality.

Articles, blogs, and social media postings on the subject have been far more prolific than books in recent years but have employed the same overall approach. This has led readers to draw conclusions that agree or disagree with what they have read, sometimes without much reflection and deliberation.

The question that sets forth the title of this book—"Is it time?"—is used in two distinct ways. The first is an extension of the title: "Is it time to stop?" It is repeated at the beginning of each of the first twelve chapters and introduces a verb that initiates the subject matter of a given chapter. The second way is a different extension of the title: "Is it time to start?" It is used only one time as an introduction to the postscript.

On the opening page for each of the twelve chapters, the words *Maybe yes . . . maybe no* follow the chapter title as an indication of openness to the response of the reader. An additional question comes after these titles: "What do you think?"

My hope is that persons who read this book will become aware of the wide variety of issues related to the subject of homosexuality, will be encouraged to reflect on each of them, will think through the meaning of whatever answers they give to the questions this book raises, will grapple with the implications of the stances they take, and will engage in conversations with others—both in a one-on-one setting and in a group.

This book is not an attempt to convert readers to my point of view. Rather, it is an effort to assist readers in understanding the issues that I and others have examined and critiqued many times. It has grown out of an intentional process, one that remains open to further development:

I study and learn.

I interact with others, especially those who have a view different from mine.

I reexamine what I think.

I follow the evidence wherever it leads.

I affirm an openness to change.

I began a time of reflection forty years ago when I was preparing to teach a college course called "The Meaning of Sex." Having taught a course titled "The Meaning of Death" several times, I learned from students that they wanted a course on human sexuality. It was the 1970s and college students across the country wanted to examine two subjects that were relatively new to college curricula: death and sex!

As part of the course on human sexuality, I included a section on homosexuality, inviting gay men and lesbian women to class—

in person and in film. I wanted students to learn from direct experiences of persons with sexual orientations other than my own. Ever since that time, and even earlier in my experiences growing up in New York City, I connected with a variety of individuals and groups who had sexual orientations different from mine.

I write from a heterosexual perspective, since that is who I am. I address issues facing the heterosexual community more fully than those facing other communities, since that is the primary context for my understanding. However, I try my best to be as sensitive as I can to represent other perspectives in as fair a manner as I know how.

The time has now come for me, an ordained elder in The United Methodist Church for more than fifty years, to attempt to contribute to the conversations taking place throughout our denomination—in this country and around the world. The time is ripe to encourage open conversation by asking questions that have sometimes been unexamined, neglected, and/or cast aside as unimportant—before official actions are taken in the coming years that might lead to irreversible consequences.

This book is structured in three parts. The first—chapters 1 through 5—considers physical and psychological issues, using terms and concepts consistent with the perspectives of the American Medical Association (AMA), the American Psychological Association (APA), and the National Association of Social Workers (NASW). The second—chapters 6 through 10—examines biblical and theological issues. The third—chapters 11 and 12—identifies relational and practical issues, connecting preceding chapters to everyday situations facing readers.

The "call" of this book is: (1) to understand more fully our own views, (2) to grasp more accurately views different from our own, (3) to follow the evidence wherever it leads, and (4) to share our thoughts and feelings with others with whom we agree and dis-agree—all in a spirit of mutual openness.

The outcome of following that "call"—hopefully—will be a time to start expending our full energy on the mission of The United Methodist Church: to make disciples of Jesus Christ for the trans-formation of the world.

NOTE: In another book by Adolf Hansen and Colleagues, *Becoming a Disciple: A Lifelong Journey* (Abingdon Press, 2015), the introduction includes the following statement:

> In the original language of Matthew 28:19—the verse in which Jesus says "Go and make disciples of all nations"—the verb *matheteuo* simply means *to disciple*. The word *make* is not in the Greek text.

Therefore, that book uses the words "to lead others to become disciples" rather than "make disciples"—a rewording offered to The UMC for consideration.

Part One

Physical and Psychological

Chapters 1–5

Is it time to stop using the word *homosexuality* without defining it?

Maybe yes. Maybe no. What do you think?

Each of us comes to the subject of homosexuality with a perspective. Some of us have a considerable level of understanding. Others have superficial knowledge, but have not explored the subject in depth. Still others have barely a limited awareness. In which group do you find yourself? Can you think of family members and friends who are in these groups?

How would you describe your background? When did you first hear about homosexuality? What were you told? Who or what was the source of the information? Can you recall details of that initial awareness—at least some of them?

How did your understanding develop after that early exposure to the subject? Can you remember the feelings you had about what you were learning? Can you identify the influences that led to them?

(pause to reflect)

Defining homosexuality isn't easy. It's more complex than a one-sentence statement. And that's why I raised the question in the title of this opening chapter: "Is it time to stop using the word *homosexuality* without defining it?"

The word *homosexuality* is a combination of a Greek word *homos* that means *same* and a Latin word *sexualis* that means *sexual*. Charles Chaddock first used it in English in 1892 in a translation of Richard von Krafft-Ebing's *Psycopathia Sexualis*. The Revised Standard Version of the Bible was the first to include it in its English translation of the New Testament in 1946; however, the word *homosexual* was removed in the 1971 edition. (Chapter 7 will explain this more fully.)

Terms that customarily relate to the subject of homosexuality include: *sex, gender, gender identity, gender role,* and *sexual orientation.* Although the word *sex* has numerous meanings, professionals in medicine, psychology, and social work commonly use the word to refer to the anatomical sex characteristics of a boy or a girl (at birth), a man or a woman (in adulthood). They use the term *gender* to refer to the behavioral and societal traits typically associated with male and female sex (e.g., masculine and feminine).

However, in ordinary speech, people often use the words *sex* and *gender* interchangeably. Those who design forms for a driver's license, an insurance application, a medical procedure, etc., might use either *sex* or *gender.* Some organizations are beginning to use the term *gender identity* on their forms.

Gender identity deals with the gender that individuals "feel" they are (i.e., their internal awareness), often the same as their biological sex, though sometimes not. In other words, a person might have been born a girl, but feels she is male; or born a boy, but feels he is female. A person whose gender identity and gender expression are completely different from society's expectation is known as a transgendered person. This means a transgendered man is a woman with a male identity, and a transgendered woman is a man with a female identity.

The term *gender role* refers to norms that society puts forward as appropriate types of behavior. They are customarily identified within categories of masculinity and femininity. However, in some situations, combinations such as these emerge: feminine woman, masculine woman, masculine man, feminine man.

Sexual orientation describes an ongoing pattern of emotional and sexual attraction to a person of the same sex or gender, the opposite sex or gender, both sexes and genders, or a lack of sexual attraction to another person. In addition, it often involves sexual activity that emerges from the attraction, as well as a sense of participation in a community of persons who share that attraction and behavior.

In the latter part of the twentieth century, *gay man* and *lesbian woman* increasingly replaced the word *homosexual*. The word *lesbian* derives from the name of the Greek island, Lesbos, where the author Sappho lived and wrote extensively about her emotional relations with women.

Although *gay* often refers to male homosexuality, it sometimes includes men and women. On occasion, it serves as an overall category for a number of non-heterosexual orientations such as those named here (and explored in subsequent chapters):

Bisexual—sexual attraction toward both men and women

Transgendered—a gender identity that differs from one's biological sex

Queer—a broader, deliberately ambiguous alternative to traditional gender terminology

Questioning—a lack of clarity about one's gender identity and/or sexual orientation

Intersexual—anatomical sex characteristics that do not fit definitions of male and female

Polyamory—intimate relations with more than one partner, with consent of all partners

Pansexual—sexual attraction to all persons regardless of sex or gender identity

Asexual—a lack of sexual attraction to other persons

It is common today to adopt an acronym—LGB, LGBT, or LGBTQ—when referring to the gay or non-heterosexual community, though some choose a more inclusive acronym such as LGBTQQIPPA.

Expressions of attraction toward and/or activity with persons of the same sex have been a part of many cultures throughout human history, though terminology has varied from place to place, and time to time. Furthermore, meanings have changed over the years. For example, some people considered homosexuality a mental illness until 1973, when the American Psychiatric Association removed it from that category. Since that time it has developed, first as an alternative lifestyle, and more recently as an expression of the full humanity of a segment of persons in society.

Increasing numbers of people, especially those with gay and related sexual orientations, have become uncomfortable with the word *homosexuality*. Reasons for this sentiment include its negative clinical history; its focus—for some people—on the sexual dimension of the relationship; its leaning toward a male perspective; its implicit exclusion of persons who are bisexual; and its many derogatory connotations.

This book, however, will use the word *homosexuality*—with apologies to those who are bothered and even offended by this term—since that is the word used throughout *The Book of Discipline of The United Methodist Church, 2016* (*BOD*), and these references constitute an essential part of the discussion. (Chapter 10 will deal with the assertion that the practice of homosexuality is "incompatible with Christian teaching.")

It is interesting that the word *homosexuality* is not defined in the *BOD*. Perhaps it ought not to be used in that volume, or in other official publications of The United Methodist Church (UMC), unless it includes a definition. In other words, the question I have raised with the readers of this book—particularly in the title of this chapter—is the same question I am raising with leaders of the UMC.

Some discussion that relates to a definition of the word *homosexuality* does appear in five decisions of the Judicial Council (JC) of the UMC, but not as a declarative definition. These decisions (numbered 764, 837, 920, 980, and 1027), dating from 1995 through 2005, speak of "genital sexual activity with a person of the same gender"—with variations in wording. (Chapter 10 will include further interpretation of these statements.)

This chapter is only the beginning of our exploration. As stepping-stones to the four chapters that follow, I invite you to reflect on the following questions: Do you agree that homosexuality contains two parts: (1) attraction to another person of the same sex, and (2) behavior that emerges from that desire? Do you distinguish between these two components? Are they separable? Do you think a person can experience the attraction without the behavior? (Chapter 2 will explore the relationship between them in greater detail.)

(pause to reflect)

Is there more to a definition of homosexuality than these two explanatory statements? For example, do you think heterosexuality and homosexuality differ from each other to the extent that they are entirely distinct from each other? Or, is there a continuum with homosexuality at one end of the spectrum, and heterosexuality at the other? Do they sometimes overlap with each other? Is this what is known as bisexuality? Furthermore, is some type of fluidity possible, so that persons might not always remain at a particular place on the spectrum throughout their lifetimes? (Chapter 3 will examine what such a continuum might entail.)

(pause to reflect)

Is there still more to consider in working out a definition of *homosexuality*? Is it important—perhaps even crucial—to distinguish between an episode and a long-term relationship? In other words, do you think homosexuality can be experienced as an event and not necessarily as an ongoing series of events? What difference would it make if you agreed with such a distinction? (Chapter 4 will analyze these possibilities.)

(pause to reflect)

In thinking through a definition of *homosexuality*, do you also need to analyze factors that contribute to a person becoming attracted to another person of the same sex? Do you think the cause is biological (i.e., genes and/or hormones)? or environmental (i.e., psychological and/or sociological)? or a matter of individual choice? Do you think it is a combination of all three? or only one or two of them? or does the cause vary from one person to the next? As you consider these options, do you have reliable data that lead you to your conclusion, or is further study needed? (Chapter 5 will explore these options.)

(pause to reflect)

Research carried out by reputable professional organizations that are not advocacy groups often conclude that 3 to 4 percent of the population in the United States is made up of homosexual persons. This means congregations that are representative of the population might have 3 or 4 persons who are homosexual in a congregation of 100 people, 17 or 18 in a congregation of 500, and 35 in a congregation of 1,000.

Homosexuality is more than an issue or a subject to define. It is a real issue, but it is also about real people. Gay men, lesbian women, and those of other sexual orientations are "individuals of sacred worth" (as stated in the *Social Principles of The United Methodist Church,* ¶161.G). They want to be treated the same as anyone else. They also want others to understand that sexuality is only one part of who they are.

QUESTIONS

1. *Have you come up with a definition of the word* homosexuality *that you can express in physical and psychological categories? If so, can you express it in one or two paragraphs? (You will have opportunity to express your thinking in biblical and theological categories in chapters 6 through 10 of Part Two.)*

2. *Would it be helpful to share your definition with someone else who is willing to listen to you? If so, who would that be?*

3. *If that person were also willing to formulate a definition and share it with you, would you be willing to listen and then exchange thoughts with each other?*

4. *Would it be worthwhile to engage in discussion with others who you think would have definitions different from your own?*

5. *As you carry out such conversations, are you learning anything new? Do these thoughts lead you to revise your initial understanding?*

6. *On the basis of your own reflections and your interactions with others, is it time to stop using the word* homosexuality *without defining it? What do you think?*

Is it time to stop confusing homosexual attraction with homosexual behavior?

Maybe yes. Maybe no. What do you think?

I was eleven years old. I had just completed the fifth grade and was looking forward to a summer of fun in the neighborhood where I lived in Brooklyn, New York.

I had many friends—some at school and some at church. I had one classmate who lived just a block away and attended the same church as I did. We went to a lot of places together, often jumping on our bikes and riding all over Brooklyn. We had one favorite place, Prospect Park, with its beautiful scenery and varied activities scattered throughout its 585 acres.

During one of our rides, we stopped to go to the bathroom—as usual—in an area of bushes and trees. But this time it turned out to be different. As we were almost finished, my friend said to me: "Let's drop our pants to the ground and see what we look like." He took off some of his clothes and, without thinking, I removed some of mine. He took a couple of steps toward me and began stroking my private parts—first in front and then in back. He then said, "You can stroke me too. Go ahead."

I touched him—both front and back—and felt uncomfortable. I wasn't sure what he had in mind. It didn't take long before I stopped, moved back a few steps, and pulled up my pants.

This was the first time and, for me, the only time I had such an encounter with another boy. I was perplexed, but I soon forgot about it as we rode off together on our bikes. However, I remembered it enough that I never again went to the bathroom in the bushes next to him.

Have you had a childhood experience that was anything similar to my experience? Those who have shared their stories with me have often said, "I think most people have had some type of homosexual experience." I have no idea if this is accurate, but I'm convinced my encounter was not a unique event.

In order to be fair, I need to add that this type of sexual encounter also happens with heterosexual individuals—probably far more often—though most persons don't share their early sexual encounters with many other people. What goes on in private situations—in homes, in schools, in other indoor locations, as well as in woods, fields, and additional outdoor locations—usually remains private. However, would it be of some value to reflect on your own early sexual encounters in order to understand more fully what took place, as well as why and how it happened? Or, for some of you, would that be too painful, particularly if you were sexually abused—heterosexually or homosexually—as a child, a youth, and/or an adult?

Understanding our own sexual desires (feelings) and behaviors (actions) is difficult enough. But to understand the experiences of others—especially when their sexual orientation or gender identity is different from our own—is often far more challenging!

The question of this chapter focuses on whether the time has come to stop confusing sexual desire with sexual behavior. Some individuals have an attraction to persons of the same sex. Where

28

does this attraction come from? Others have an attraction to persons of the opposite sex. Where does this attraction come from? Are such desires God-given? If they are, does it follow that homosexual as well as heterosexual desires come from God?

(pause to reflect)

The Judicial Council (JC) of The United Methodist Church (UMC) has made the distinction between homosexual desire and behavior. In one of its decisions (544), the JC states that "¶402.2 . . . does not per se bar homosexual persons from the ordained ministry of The United Methodist Church." It goes on to say that this paragraph "is directed toward those persons who are 'self-avowed practicing homosexuals,' which is an entirely different matter." In other words, individuals with a homosexual attraction might be ordained in the UMC just as those with a heterosexual attraction. Another decision of the JC (1027) states the same view unequivocally: "No provision of the *Discipline* bars a person with a same-sex orientation from the ordained ministry of The United Methodist Church."

The statement of the JC seems to avoid confusion when it comes to the difference between attraction and behavior, even using the words *same-sex orientation* in the description of same-sex attraction. Do you agree with what the JC has declared? If so, is this an understanding that separates desire from activity—attraction from behavior—rather than confusing the two? (Chapter 10 will explore the phrase "self-avowed practicing homosexual.")

(pause to reflect)

Behavior of persons engaging in sexual activity with those of the same sex varies in many ways that are personal and complex—just like behavior of heterosexual individuals. Nevertheless, clarifying some generalities might be useful. Otherwise, we might make assumptions about what we don't know and might be incorrect in more ways than we realize.

Meaningful sexual activity between gay men or lesbian women takes place in the context of a relationship of mutual respect, caring, and trust—just like meaningful sexual activity between heterosexuals (an understanding that we will explore more fully in chapter 4).

How a heterosexual man and a heterosexual woman carry out their sexual behavior is an understanding I can readily describe, since that is my sexual orientation. Activities that are common include: hugging, kissing, fondling, fingering, and intercourse. Some heterosexual couples also engage in additional activities such as oral sex and other stimulating experiences.

Within homosexual relationships there are behaviors that might not easily be understood. How gay men carry out their sexual activity is not an understanding I can readily describe for a number of reasons. However, in numerous conversations I have had with heterosexual men and women, there is an assumption that is often made, namely that the primary means of sexual activity between two gay men is anal intercourse. Unable to locate reliable data on this matter, I asked a social acquaintance who is remarkably knowledgeable of persons in the gay community: "How common is anal intercourse among gay men?"

"As far as I'm aware," he answered, "it's about as common for gay men as it is for straight men."

"I don't believe anal intercourse is very common among straight men," I responded.

He then said, "Well, does that answer your question?"

Gay men carry out their sexual behavior with other men in a

variety of ways—some of them not that different from activities carried out by heterosexual couples: hugging, kissing, fondling, and fingering. Some gay men also engage in other experiences such as oral sex, frotting (rubbing one's penis against a partner's penis), intercrural sex (placing one's penis between a partner's thighs and thrusting to create friction), and anal sex.

Lesbian women carry out their sexual behavior with other women in a variety of ways—some of them similar to experiences that take place among heterosexual couples: hugging, kissing, fondling, and fingering. Some lesbian women also participate in activities such as oral sex, tribbing (rubbing one's vulva against a partner's vulva, or other body part), and the use of dildos (sex toys, often phallic in appearance).

At the heart of intimate sexual activity is the pleasurable experience of *orgasm*. Since this is a natural physiological response for most individuals, is it an experience created by God when God created human beings? When a boy has a nighttime emission known as a *wet dream* in early adolescence (waking up to wet semen he has ejaculated), is this a God-given experience? When a girl experiences an emission known as *vaginal wetness*, is this a God-given experience?

Closely related to orgasm is *masturbation*—a boy or girl, man or woman, stimulating himself or herself by sight, sound, and/or touch to reach a climactic orgasm; or being stimulated by someone else—individually (as a recipient) or mutually (as a participant). Since this is a natural and pleasurable experience for most human beings, is there anything wrong with it when carried out in a reasonable, thoughtful, respectful manner? Is it a God-given possibility?

Is the story of Onan in Genesis 38:1-10 about masturbation? Or is it about fulfilling the laws of levirate marriage, in which a man is obligated to impregnate his brother's widow in order that she might produce descendants? According to the story, God reprimanded Onan and killed him because "he spilled his semen on the ground . . . so that he would not give offspring to his brother" (verse 9). Is it a misunderstanding to interpret this story as a prohibition of masturbation?

Furthermore, in the world of the Old and New Testaments, the predominant biological understanding was that the man had the *seed* and the woman was the *receptacle*. People in that day did not understand that a woman typically has two X chromosomes, and a man typically has one X and one Y chromosome; and that one chromosome from a woman, and one from a man, is the basis for procreation.

As far as we can determine, orgasm was common to heterosexuals and homosexuals in *that* day, as it is in *our* day. It was—and is—one of the pleasurable goals of sexual activity, and can be achieved by oneself, together with a person of a different sex, or together with a person of the same sex. Is it a common experience that all human beings seek? Is it most meaningful when it grows out of an intimate relationship of two people who love each other deeply and faithfully, whether they are heterosexual or homosexual?

(pause to reflect)

Interpreting sexual behavior is more difficult when we consider persons who have a bodily limitation. Included in this context are individuals: (1) who are ill; (2) who have lost a body part or function; (3) who are struggling with an emotional or mental illness; (4) who are addicted to alcohol or drugs; (5) who are older, weak, and feeble; and (6) who have other similar challenges.

Understanding sexual behavior is not easy. Neither is thinking about it, nor writing about it. Yet, it seems to me, it is essential if we are going to discuss—honestly and candidly—what we think about it, and how we feel about it.

I ask you not to reject consideration of the varied dimensions of sexual attraction and behavior, and not to turn away from candidly discussing what might be uncomfortable. It might be that God is trying to help us be more open and gracious with each other.

QUESTIONS

1. Do you remember sexual experiences you had as a child? What are your thoughts and feelings about them now?

2. How do you distinguish between sexual attraction and behavior? In what ways do you understand their similarities and differences?

3. What are you learning about sexual activities of persons with an orientation or identity different from your own?

4. Do you think orgasm is a natural and pleasurable experience for human beings? Is it a part of God's creation?

5. In responding to these questions, are there some answers that you regard as personal and private, and want to keep to yourself? Are there other answers you are willing to share?

6. On the basis of your own reflections and your interactions with others, is it time to stop confusing homosexual desire with homosexual behavior? What do you think?

Is it time to stop thinking categories of sexual orientation such as heterosexual and homosexual are separate from each other rather than a continuum from one to the other?

Maybe yes. Maybe no. What do you think?

I didn't know her, but I knew her brother. We were faculty members at the same university.

One morning as we were sipping a cup of coffee in the student center, he told me about a letter he had just received from his younger sister in San Francisco. "I can hardly believe what she told me. She's getting married to a man and wants me to come to California for the wedding in August."

"Why is that surprising?" I asked.

"I'm stunned," he responded. "She left home right after graduating from high school—almost ten years ago. She was a loner—didn't date any of the guys—didn't get along with Mom and Dad.

She actually became so angry with my dad during her teenage years that she didn't want to talk to him, or ever see him."

As we continued the conversation, my colleague told me about his dad, a man who was abusive to him and his younger sister—verbally, emotionally, physically. He also revealed that his dad had sexually abused his sister—first as a little girl and then more intensely when she became a teenager—although he didn't know about that abuse until he was about to leave for college. He felt terrible about it, but he didn't know what to do.

My colleague also told me he hadn't seen his sister since she had moved and hadn't heard from her except for her note on the annual Christmas card. He did learn that she and another woman had become "partners," a woman who really loved her, and whom she really loved. But now she was going to get married to a man.

"Is she attracted to women and to men?" I asked.

He responded and said, "I really don't know. I'm going to have some long talks with her when I see her."

My colleague moved to another university a few months later and, though we met occasionally at professional meetings, I never learned the rest of the story. Was his sister a heterosexual woman who turned away from boys and men because she was experiencing sexual abuse by her father? Or was she a lesbian woman who had finally learned who she was when she found a female partner? Or was she a bisexual woman, attracted to both women and men?

The American Psychological Association and a number of other professional organizations claim sexual orientation exists along a continuum, with heterosexuality at one end, and homosexuality at the other. Although most people identify with one of these orientations, others identify themselves as bisexual—somewhere between the two. Still others think of themselves as primarily one or the other orientation, but not 100 percent. They think of their orientation in terms of percentages (i.e., 90 to 95, 80 to 85, etc., toward one end of the continuum).

(pause to reflect)

Bisexual persons dislike the terms *homosexual* and *hetero-sexual*, since they consider themselves neither one. They think of themselves—in different ways—as being *both/and* rather than *either/or*. They might identify with both ends of the spectrum at the same time—in attraction only, or in both attraction and behavior—or might identify with homosexual or heterosexual individuals at certain times, or in particular situations, or at various stages of their lives—or, at all times.

Some persons who are attracted to homosexual and heterosexual orientations are known as *two-spirit* individuals. They are commonly part of a Native American tribe. The precise name they use varies according to the language they speak. The term *two-spirit* is an umbrella term to enable outsiders to understand who they are and how they function.

These designated individuals have particular roles within their respective communities. In addition to categories of male and female, some are known as *two-spirit males* or *two-spirit females*. They are often thought to be sacred and are highly revered. They have the capacity to use two sides of their humanity and are therefore regarded as endowed with special gifts. Their prominence, however, has been substantially reduced over the years as a result of European assumptions that often limit individuals to function as males or females.

Some cultures beyond the United States and Europe refer to more than two genders. They sometimes speak of *three-gender* people, or as many as *five-gender* people.

In addition to thinking about possibilities along a continuum, is it important to consider potential movement between those possibilities—what some people call *fluidity*? Although most people seem to be fairly firm in their sexual orientation, some move from one to another—not necessarily from one end of the spectrum to the other, but from one end to somewhere near the middle; or from somewhere close to the middle to one of the more exclusive orientations. Though attractions commonly remain firm, can identities and/or behaviors fluctuate?

(pause to reflect)

Whether sexual orientations can change has been a hotly debated issue. Some who reject homosexuality have supported—and sometimes eagerly carried out—actions that might lead individuals (especially gay men) to experience a *conversion* that would lead them to a heterosexual orientation. An organization known as Exodus International promoted a path away from homosexuality that—for more than thirty years—included the possibility of reversal in orientation in the form of a *cure*. However, that has changed; its leaders no longer believes as they did; and in 2013 Exodus shut down and publicly apologized, especially to the gay community, for the misinformation it promulgated, and the hurtful impact it had.

Organizations such as the American Medical Association and the American Psychological Association oppose therapeutic approaches that claim homosexuality can be cured. Furthermore, in April 2017 the governor of New Mexico signed legislation protecting LGBTQ youth from *conversion therapy*. In May 2017 the Supreme Court of the United States rejected—for the third time—a challenge to California's 2012 law that protects LGBTQ youth from *conversion therapy*—also called *sexual orientation change effort,* or *reparative therapy.* Do you agree that this type of *conversion therapy* is inappropriate?

Individuals at varying ages sometimes struggle with their sexual orientation, especially during childhood, teenage, and young adult years. They have many questions and often are not sure with whom they can speak. They might not feel comfortable approaching parents, teachers, and other authority figures in the church and community. They more often seek conversations with older siblings and friends their own age, though hesitation often occurs—for a number of reasons. They commonly peruse websites and other online resources, but often find so much information and such conflicting data that the end result is confusion. Even more problematical are the multitude of feelings that emerge, with few if any persons with whom to process them—leading many to subscribe to a *questioning* orientation.

Some persons who become uncertain about their own sexual orientation find themselves resonating with a *pansexual* identity (*pan,* a Greek word for *all*). They think and feel they don't have to choose a particular sexuality or identity. As a result, they embrace a variety of sexual activities along the continuum of heterosexuality/bisexuality/homosexuality, or in directions that do not fit within such a binary spectrum.

Whatever your sexual orientation, have you thought about questions that pertain to it? For example, if you are heterosexual: (1) How did you first learn you were heterosexual? (2) Is it something you chose? (3) At what age did this take place? (4) To whom did you disclose this orientation, or at least tendencies in this direction? (5) How did these other persons react to you?

On the other hand, if you are homosexual or bisexual: How would you answer the same questions?

My assumption is that these questions are more commonly asked of gay men, lesbian women, and bisexual individuals. But when asked of heterosexual men and women, do insights emerge that are helpful to your understanding and awareness?

(pause to reflect)

When you think about matters that might not be familiar to you—at least not in detail—how do you react? Are you drawn by a desire to learn more? or a desire to shift to something more familiar? or a fluctuation between the two?

Likewise, when you are in touch with your feelings about such matters, do they energize you, put you at ease, or stir you with feelings of uncertainty, apprehension, and agitation—even fear?

QUESTIONS

1. When you started to read this chapter, were you thinking of heterosexuality and homosexuality as exclusive categories—totally separate from each other? If you were, do you still think that way?

2. Whether or not you agree, how do you understand the point of view that thinks of sexual orientation as a continuum?

3. Do you know persons who adhere to each of these points of view? Would you find it helpful to discuss these possibilities, particularly with someone who would affirm a perspective other than your own?

4. What is your understanding of bisexuality? Is this your sexual orientation? If not, have you had conversations with individuals who identify themselves in this way? If so, what did you learn? If not, are you willing to locate such persons and have the type of conversations with them that will enable you to learn from them?

5. In what ways did you grow in your understanding as you read this chapter? Would you find it helpful to share your thoughts and feelings with someone else?

6. On the basis of your own reflections and your interactions with others, is it time to stop thinking that categories of sexual orientation such as heterosexual and homosexual are separate from each other rather than a continuum from one to the other? What do you think?

Is it time to stop misunderstanding the difference between an episode and a long-term relationship?

Maybe yes. Maybe no. What do you think?

It was a pleasant fall evening in midtown Manhattan. I was walking along Third Avenue when I noticed a smartly dressed man on my left turn toward me, smile, and in a crisp British accent say, "Good evening!" I responded with the same greeting.

We were coming to the corner just as the light was turning red. He continued the conversation by saying: "I'm visiting New York for the first time and need some help with directions." That's a common way to get New Yorkers to stop and talk. For some it's the only way a person will stop and talk to a stranger.

After I answered a couple of questions, he somewhat abruptly changed the subject, looked directly into my eyes and simply said, "I'm in New York for pleasure . . . as well as business." And before I could respond, he simply said, "You, too?"

I was tempted to say, "What did you have in mind?" But I knew I was likely to get an invitation to go with him for a drink—perhaps in his hotel room. I simply said, "Not me," and crossed the street as the light turned green.

Receiving those types of invitations—for what is often known as a "trick"—was not uncommon in the neighborhood where I lived at the time. As a matter of fact, just a few buildings from my apartment was a refined-looking store, with large glass panels covering almost the entire front, except for a single door at one side. The display behind the glass consisted of white satin sheets from the top of the display to the bottom. Draped among the folds were numerous figurines and flowers—classic male statues in stone, together with cupids and other statuary. The sign above the front of the store read "Maness House."

It didn't take many passes by that store to conclude what it was. After conferring with others who lived in the same apartment building as I did, I became aware that the store was the headquarters for gay men in the area.

Heterosexual women on the street also approached me—more often than men. Sometimes they simply walked up to me. At other times they gestured to me while sitting on an open windowsill or standing behind a large glass window—sometimes naked, or nearly so. On one fall evening in another city, an attractive woman in a fur coat sauntered over to a colleague and me, pulled her coat apart to reveal her nude body, and simply said, "Interested?" I don't remember what we said, but I do remember we walked away rather quickly.

These are some of the episodic encounters in my life, though others have been more sophisticated—those that usually take more time to develop yet end up at the same destination. Have you had similar experiences, whether initiated in a brief moment, or over a longer period of time? Have you been approached by a man or a woman of a different sexual orientation? Or someone of your own orientation?

Episodes take place in many ways that are not a part of a long-term relationship. They sometimes take place at the beginning of a long-term relationship. At other times, they function in the form of an experiment in which a person explores possibilities out of curiosity.

At still other times, they involve promiscuous behavior, characterized by indiscriminate sexual encounters, including sexual activity with one person or a number of partners on a casual, haphazard basis. In these circumstances, persons often use each other for their own pleasure and gain. Their activities are commonly described as licentious, loose, and unchaste behaviors.

The incidents I have described are voluntary, not coercive. They come about by choice, not force. They are not like sexual abuse, rape, or other forced sexual assault. Such experiences, and others like them, are horrible—often so horrible that they are almost impossible to put into words. Although incredibly important to consider, they are beyond the scope of this book.

In my younger years, I was aware of episodic events that took place between two men or between a man and a woman, but I was not aware of episodic events between two women. One of the reasons is obvious: I'm a man. But another reason came from my understanding of certain differences between a man and a woman. Generally speaking, a man's sexual arousal can be very rapid. Sometimes it only takes a matter of seconds for an erection to occur. And, on occasion, it only takes a matter of minutes before an orgasm occurs—especially in adolescent boys and younger men. In addition, a man often thinks about sex. When he urinates, he usually holds his penis in his hand, and then squeezes it or shakes it when he is finished. A woman usually uses toilet paper and doesn't have to physically touch her genital area at all.

Is this the way God has made men and women? If so, is it okay to talk about it?

(pause to reflect)

Episodic events for men who are promiscuous often include genital contact, whether the experience is with another man or a woman. On the other hand, episodic events for women who are promiscuous often include genital contact when they are with a man initially, but often times not when they are with a woman initially. Although this borders on being an oversimplification, men sometimes begin with sexual activity and then—perhaps—move on to develop a meaningful relationship; while women sometimes begin with developing a meaningful relationship and then—perhaps—move on to sexual activity.

For a long time I had limited awareness of long-term relationships between persons with the same sexual orientation. Perhaps this was simply not a part of my earlier experience. However, I also realize it might have been long enough ago—for me the 1960s—that such ongoing relationships were not public information on a large scale.

What experiences have you had over the years with people you've met who have a sexual orientation different from your own? Did you learn about episodic events? Did you become aware of long-term relationships? Did you also get to know some of these individuals in a personal manner?

(pause to reflect)

Today, more than ever, two women or two men, as well as a man and a woman, yearn for deep and lasting commitments. They have increasingly come to realize—personally or through what others have told them—that incidents are often less satisfying and less meaningful than they had imagined, especially when the reality sets in that the pleasure was momentary and the connection was shallow.

The difference between an episodic event and a long-term relationship is often misunderstood, particularly when they are not distinguished from each other. This seems particularly true when persons think about sexual orientations other than their own. For example, a straight person might assume that a connection between two men is an incident, apart from any ongoing commitment. Likewise, a straight person might assume the same perspective regarding two women. (Chapter 7 will explore particular biblical passages to determine if they are references to a long-term commitment or an episode.)

When two people make a commitment to be faithful to each other and then live out this commitment, how are their lifestyles different from those who live a promiscuous way of life? Is there a different kind of relationship when a man and a woman mutually agree to refrain from sexual intimacy with any other person? Is there a different kind of relationship when two women, or two men, make the same type of commitment? Are such monogamous relationships—over time—ones that likely will increase in depth and sustainability? Is marriage a confirmation of the lifetime commitment of such an ongoing relationship? Is there any way other than marriage to express such a lifetime commitment?

(pause to reflect)

A primary reason for a man and a woman to marry is the bearing of children through their own procreation. And that is incredibly satisfying and meaningful for heterosexual couples who are able to have children. Is a similar experience available for a single woman or man? or two women? or two men? or a man and a woman?—when there is an adoption, or when pregnancy takes place by artificial insemination?

Are there also other reasons for marriage between a man and a woman, or two women, or two men? Do some of these reasons include the possibility of filing joint income taxes? the opportunity for inclusion in certain financial benefits such as an inheritance? the right to function as the next of kin when dealing with lawful claims such as guardian relationships and powers of attorney and medical situations that warrant actions on behalf of another in times of illness, near death, at death, and/or after death? or, more simply, the desire to express respect, commitment, faithfulness, intimacy, and mutual love?

Sometimes mutual commitments do not remain solid. Sometimes they weaken; at other times they break. Sometimes they're temporary; at other times they're permanent. Divorce sometimes occurs when the differences become irreconcilable. Is the situation similar when two persons with the same sexual orientation make a commitment to be faithful to each other and then—later on—find their relationship weakening and sometimes breaking?

For more than seventy-five years Harvard University has conducted two longitudinal studies that tracked the physical and emotional well-being of two groups. One, the Grant Study, monitored 456 men growing up in Boston from 1939 through 2014. The other, the Glueck Study, followed 268 undergraduates who attended Harvard from 1930 through 1944. According to the various directors of these studies over the years, the thing that has stood out with more importance than any other is "good relationships." They keep people happier and healthier than anything else—more than education, wealth, recognitions, and opportunities to exercise power. The directors of these studies summarize this in the word *love,* particularly when they combine this word with finding ways of coping that does not push love away.

QUESTIONS

1. *What is your understanding of the difference between episodic and long-term relationships?*

2. *When did you first learn about two women or two men living in a long-term committed relationship?*

3. *How did you learn about them? Did it include learning from them?*

4. *Are good relationships—however you define these words—at the heart of fulfillment in our lives, whatever our sexual orientation? If so, what do these relationships look like in everyday life? What fosters their growth? What hinders their ongoing development?*

5. *Do you want to discuss thoughts from this chapter with another individual? If so, what are those thoughts, and who is that person?*

6. *On the basis of your own reflections and your interactions with others, is it time to stop misunderstanding the difference between an episode and a long-term relationship? What do you think?*

Is it time to stop claiming homosexuality is strictly biological, or environmental, or a matter of choice?

Maybe yes. Maybe no. What do you think?

When I was a university faculty member, I met a well-educated man from the community who frequently attended university programs open to the public. With my office on a corridor, and with my door ajar during the latter part of certain afternoons, he would occasionally stop by for conversation on a variety of subjects. We enjoyed each other's company.

One day, as we were discussing what our respective employment entailed, he got my attention when he said he spent a lot of time with men—often in evening hours. I didn't know what he meant, so I asked him about it. He startled me with his answer when he said, "I meet with men individually, in private settings."

"And . . . ," I said.

He was quick to respond with these words: "I service men— married as well as single. They tell me I'm really good at it."

All of a sudden I realized what he meant. And before I could respond, he simply asked: "Are you interested?"

I don't remember what I said, but I spoke firmly, yet graciously, and indicated that I had no need for his service and that I was a happily married man. He then apologized for his inquiry, but asked if we could still continue our conversations. I agreed on one condition, namely, that he would not make such an inquiry again. He immediately said, "Yes, of course."

In the months that followed I learned much about him as a gay man, the community of which he was a part, and his understanding of what it meant to be gay. This included discussions of what led him—as well as others—to affirm a homosexual orientation. He would often come back to the same words: "I'm really not sure."

Most professionals in medical, psychological, and social work fields do not think sexual orientation is the result of any one factor. They commonly include two primary causes: biological and environmental. Yet they differentiate particular determinants in their studies.

Some professionals focus predominantly on biological factors. Although no one among them claims there is a gay gene, they often say that genes play a role. Studies of gay brothers suggest that a specific stretch of the X chromosome might have a gene that predisposes a boy to being gay; however, others are skeptical of such studies since the number of those who have been tested is small, and results have been difficult to replicate.

Not all studies of homosexuality center on boys. Some studies of identical twin girls show a higher percentage of homosexuality. Still, fewer than half share their sister's sexual orientation. In addition, genetic linkage techniques that identify only broad regions that contain numerous genes have given way to genome-wide association studies that permit a gene to be related to a particular trait.

The emerging field of epigenetics examines the external modifications that might be made to DNA and, as a result, turn certain genes *on* and *off*, both inside and outside the womb. For example, one hormone that mimics testosterone—though in a much weaker manner—might influence a male fetus to become more predisposed toward becoming homosexual.

Some brain studies have also produced intriguing results. With the use of resonance imaging to compare the symmetry of the brains of persons who are straight and others who are gay, the data in one study showed unexpected outcomes. Brains of gay men had a tendency to resemble those of straight women rather than straight men. Brains of gay women in the study had a tendency to look like those of straight men more than straight women.

Many professionals in these fields believe there is evidence in genetic, hormonal, and brain structure variations; however, they do not claim that heredity demonstrates a clear and direct correlation. Neither do they say that the data on which they base their interpretations are conclusive, since human beings are highly complex.

What is your impression of such studies and others you might have read? Which ones interest you the most?

(pause to reflect)

Other professionals are more inclined to look at environmental factors, often paying attention to the mother, and/or other members of the immediate family. One consideration is the effect of the fraternal birth order, namely, that the greater number of older biological brothers a boy has, the higher the likelihood he might be gay. Support for this has come from the possibility that the mother's body builds up an immune assault on the fetus of her son. With certain antigens not functioning properly, the heterosexual signal in the brain sometimes has difficulty developing. And such a condition might further increase with each son born. However, this analysis has limited evidence in support of it.

In addition to members of a person's immediate family, some professionals explore parent-child relationships. They affirm—in large numbers—that most children raised by lesbian and gay parents turn out to be heterosexual. In addition, they state that most gay and lesbian adults were raised by heterosexual parents.

However, the influence of primary caregivers in the early development of a child (mother, father, siblings, grandparents, and other child-care individuals) is significant for the development of any child, regardless of whatever sexual orientation emerges. Nevertheless, those relationships—whether basically positive or negative—do not in themselves determine sexual orientation.

The relationships in which an infant/child/adolescent engages—whether male or female—involves a large number of variables. The development of attachments to particular persons, places, events, things, and other intangibles are not only difficult to discern, but even harder to comprehend when analyzed in terms of the causal connections between them. Furthermore, the effects that emerge from these interactions are not easily related to the development of an individual's sexual orientation. Nevertheless, there is common agreement that tendencies toward homosexuality often begin at an early age, though sometimes not expressed or understood.

Another environmental factor involves the gender nonconformity of some children who are inclined toward activities that are typical of the opposite sex rather than their own. In other words, a gender nonconforming boy might prefer activities of girls. Or, a gender nonconforming girl might be interested in those things that boys customarily do. These inclinations sometimes lead children to feel different from other children of their own sex, and more comfortable with persons of the opposite sex.

Additional environmental influences that are sometimes identified include the sociological setting in which a child grows up. Some studies of large urban areas claim that such settings are more conducive to predisposing children—particularly boys—to homosexuality. Other studies identify particular cultural norms prevalent in a person's childhood and adolescent years.

What do you think of such studies and others you might have read? Which ones seem most valid?

(pause to reflect)

Most professionals dealing with the physical and psychological dimensions of homosexuality do not regard choice as a primary cause. However, they leave room for some influence coming from choices made by lesbian women, gay men, or persons with other sexual orientations or gender identities, especially at earlier times in their lives.

These professionals sometimes speak of an *interplay* of primary factors as the cause of homosexuality. In other words, they affirm that interactions occur between biological and environmental causes. In addition, they leave room—though limited in scope—for the interaction of the individual with these primary factors. Do you agree with this approach?

(pause to reflect)

A small number of professionals say the cause of homosexuality is strictly biological. Likewise, a small group says it is exclusively environmental. But almost none say it is solely a matter of choice. Are such limited perspectives based on an affirmation of only some of the evidence? Are they, or individuals who use the phrase "born this way," defining the cause of homosexuality in a way that is too simplistic? Is searching for the cause more complex?

I find the process of learning one of the most significant dimensions of my life. It keeps me from getting old. Yes, I get older each year, but I never stop learning. Every day I look forward to growth in understanding myself, other people similar to me and—more importantly—different from me. And even more crucial, I yearn for the leading of the Holy Spirit in all I attempt to learn.

I am not an expert on the physical and psychological dimensions of homosexuality; but I have learned, and I continue to learn. I invite you to join me—and many others—in this venture.

QUESTIONS

1. *Were you thinking of one cause of homosexuality when you started reading this chapter? If you were, do you still think that way?*

2. *In your understanding of the causes of homosexuality, what evidence do you think supports the biological factor?*

3. *In your understanding of the causes of homosexuality, what evidence do you think supports the environmental factor?*

4. *In your understanding of the causes of homosexuality, what evidence do you think supports the choice factor?*

5. *Do you know a homosexual person with whom you could have a discussion regarding the causes of homosexuality? If so, are you willing to take the initiative and set up a time to meet with that person?*

6. *On the basis of your own reflections and your interactions with others, is it time to stop claiming homosexuality is strictly biological, or environmental, or a matter of choice? What do you think?*

Part Two

Biblical and Theological

Chapters 6–10

Is it time to stop interpreting the Bible as a static rather than a developing understanding of God's revelation?

Maybe yes. Maybe no. What do you think?

When I was a student at Taylor University in Upland, Indiana, I became acquainted with Milo Rediger, not only as the academic dean who taught one or two classes a year, but as an inspiring presence on campus!

Many students who had gotten to know him spoke so highly of him and shared how life-changing it was to take a class with him. I signed up for his class, Old Testament Literature, as soon as I could. The class—more specifically, the professor—created a learning environment that replaced the fear of learning new concepts with a calmness that was anchored in trust. Yes, I grew to trust the professor; but more than this, I grew to trust my capacity to reason—deeply, fairly, and thoroughly!

At the heart of my trust was a profound acceptance of one of Dr. Rediger's assumptions: *You don't have to be afraid of truth— whenever and however you find it—because God is the source of all truth.* Internalizing that statement allowed me to ask any and all questions, to examine data wherever I might find it, and to draw conclusions on whatever evidence I found. I became *free* to explore and discover truth and to never be afraid of where that would lead me, because I would always be led to God, not away from God. Why? Because I had learned God was the source of all truth!

One of the new ideas for me was a question that surfaced in class one day: "Does the Bible set forth an unfolding revelation of God?" What that meant, I learned, was a way of looking at the Bible as a developing understanding of God's revelation, rather than a static comprehension that writers of biblical books had. In other words, does the Bible contain an understanding of God's revelation that moves forward with an increasing level of clarity?

In addition, I learned that a developing understanding of God's revelation emerged within the life of a community of people, not solely within an individual—a community that had a history, a set of traditions, a culture, a belief system, and a series of practices. First, it was the Israelite community, and later the Christian community.

The first five books of the Hebrew Bible—often identified as the Pentateuch or the Torah—contain examples of this understanding. Although they were composed in a world of polytheism (i.e., many gods), they didn't exemplify that understanding. But did they set forth a developed understanding of monotheism? Or did they first express a belief in henotheism (i.e., one god above the other gods)?

Numerous passages in the Pentateuch illustrate the basis for the question. Examples include passages such as Exodus 15:11, "Who is like you, O Lord, among the gods?" and Deuteronomy 5:7, "You shall have no other gods before me" [or "besides me"]. Verses such as these do not deny the existence of other gods, but affirm the exclusivity of Israel's loyalty to one God. This understanding becomes universal in later prophecy. Zechariah, a prophet who lived centuries later, gives one illustration—among many—of a more developed understanding of God when he says, "And the LORD will become king over all the earth; on the day the LORD will be one and his name one" (14:9).

Henotheism, or the variation known as *monolatrism* (the belief in the existence of many gods, but with worship of only one deity) is also a part of this unfolding; however, such a view is simply an attempt to explain how the thinking of the Hebrew people moved from polytheism to monotheism. Even the *shema* of the Jewish people fits in with such an understanding: "Hear, O Israel: Yahweh" [a Hebrew name translated with a capital L and the letters ORD in small caps in the NRSV and other translations] "is our God, Yahweh alone. You shall love Yahweh your God with all your heart, and with all your soul, and with all your might" (Deuteronomy 6:4-5). Likewise, Joshua exhorts the people by saying: "If you are unwilling to serve Yahweh, choose this day whom you will serve, whether the gods your ancestors served in the region beyond the River or the gods of the Amorites in whose land you are living; but as for me and my household, we will serve Yahweh (24:15)."

The New Testament contains a further unfolding of monotheism, an understanding that includes an affirmation of a triune Godhead, though it is not as fully developed as it will become in the Councils of Nicaea (325), Constantinople (381), Ephesus (431), and Chalcedon (451). Nevertheless, several passages make reference to God the Father, the Lord Jesus Christ, and the Holy Spirit. For example, Paul writes in 2 Corinthians 13:13: "The grace of the Lord Jesus Christ, the love of God, and the communion of the Holy Spirit be with all of you." In addition, the writer of the Gospel according to John—as well as others—provides a lengthy exposition of the relationships between the three persons of the Trinity (14:1-31).

A second example of a developing understanding *within* the Bible relates to marriage. In a number of passages in the Old Testament, a man had a wife and a concubine—a woman who lived with a man, had sex with him, and bore him children. This woman, usually with a lower social status, was not given the status of a wife because that would have given her property rights—a central reason for marriage.

Numerous references contain the names of the husband and his concubine: Nahor (Absalom's brother) had Reumah (Genesis 22:23-24); Jacob had Bilhah (Genesis 35:22); and Saul had Rizpah (2 Samuel 3:7). Other leaders of the Hebrew people had concubines, though they remain nameless: Abraham (1 Chronicles 1:32), and Gideon, who also had "many wives" (Judges 8:30). David had "more concubines and wives" (2 Samuel 5:13). And, Rehoboam had "eighteen wives and sixty concubines" (2 Chronicles 11:21).

What do these references say about sexual relations in the Bible? What do they say about multiple wives? What definition of marriage grows out of these passages? And what further interpretation of marriage emerges in the New Testament? (See chapter 9 for additional analysis.) Is this evidence of a developing understanding of God's revelation *within* the Bible?

(pause to reflect)

Is there also evidence of a developing understanding *within and beyond* the Bible? Are the role of women in the church and the role of slavery in society readily identifiable examples of this assertion?

One of the passages pertaining to women is 1 Corinthians 14:33-35: "As in all the churches of the saints, women should be silent in the churches. For they are not permitted to speak, but should be subordinate, as the law also says. If there is anything they desire to know, let them ask their husbands at home. For it is shameful for a woman to speak in church." The footnote in the NRSV states: "Other ancient authorities put verses 34-35 after verse 40" (the end of the chapter). The word *authorities* refers primarily to extant manuscripts. And in this instance, those manuscripts are few in number, date from the sixth and ninth centuries, and are considered by scholars as considerably less reliable. Nevertheless, wherever a manuscript includes these verses, they are still a part of 1 Corinthians 14.

Another reference is 1 Timothy 2:11-12: "Let a woman learn in silence with full submission. I permit no woman to teach or have authority over a man; she is to keep silent." The translation of the Greek word *gune* is *woman* or *wife*. Likewise, the translation of the Greek word *aner* is *man* or *husband*. There is no textual variant in these two verses.

In each of these passages, Paul (or, in the case of First Timothy, a letter that might have been written in Paul's name after his death) states the customary cultural practices of the times. However, in Galatians 3:28, Paul states: "There is no longer Jew or Greek, there is no longer slave or free, there is no longer male and female; for all of you are one in Christ Jesus." Had Paul not gained that insight, the role of women in the United States (and elsewhere) might not have received this glimpse of truth for some time to come. For it is the only definitive statement on these matters in all his letters.

However, that unfolding awareness might not have come to fruition when it did without such a verse. Yes, nineteen centuries is a very long time; but it might have been longer had not that insight of equality been so clearly expressed.

A second example of a developing understanding of God's revelation *within and beyond* the Bible deals with slavery. One passage is Ephesians 6:5-6: "Slaves, obey your earthly masters with fear and trembling, in singleness of heart, as you obey Christ; not only while being watched, and in order to please them, but as slaves of Christ, doing the will of God from the heart."

The emancipation of slaves in the United States (and elsewhere) is similar to the emergence of the role of women through the centuries. However, this matter is different, since various societies structured their slavery into their own systems. Though movements of freedom emerged at different times and places, it took the Civil War to begin to break the bonds of slavery in the United States. And yet, a century and a half later, many systems and structures of society in the United States continue to be racist—some even more insidious than ever since racism is so deeply engrained systemically.

Are these two examples evidence of a developing understanding of God's revelation *within and beyond* the Bible?

(pause to reflect)

Is there also evidence of a developing understanding of God's revelation *beyond* the Bible? One example is the *implicit* understanding of the last part of Galatians 3:28: "All of you are one in Christ Jesus." The affirmation also appears in 3:26: "In Christ Jesus you are all children of God through faith." In addition, countless other New Testament passages reiterate the same truth.

The only time Paul does not refer to the recipients of one of his letters as a singular "church" is when he addresses "the churches of Galatia." This is not surprising since Galatia was a large Roman province in central Asia Minor (i.e., present-day Turkey). And it would also not be surprising that these congregations would include a variety of followers of Jesus Christ, though the message of the gospel—particularly its implications regarding circumcision—

would not yet be very clear to many of the people in the churches. It was simply too early in the emerging missionary movement (the late 40s and early 50s of the first century).

The ministry in this geographical region was extensive (Acts 13:13–14:28), and the response from people at times overwhelming. At one location, "almost the whole city gathered to hear the word of the Lord" (13:44).

How diversified were the throngs of people in "the churches of Galatia"? That's difficult to say, but a number of possibilities exist: citizenship, language, level of education, color of skin, cultural identification, physical/mental/emotional health, level of wealth or depth of poverty, religious heritage, and sexual orientation. Could it be that all of these variations are implicitly included in Paul's affirmation: "All of you are one in Christ Jesus?"

A second example that is *beyond* the Bible is the matter of divorce (a subject that will be explored more fully in chapter 9). One example is Mark 10:1-12, where Jesus says: "Whoever divorces his wife and marries another commits adultery against her" (10:11). Yet the understanding that has developed, particularly in The United Methodist Church, is that divorce is acceptable for laypeople and ordained clergy, even for leaders such as denominational executives, district superintendents, and bishops. Is it accurate to say that an understanding stated in the Bible—even by Jesus himself—has not only been modified, but reversed? Is this clear evidence of a developing understanding of God's revelation *beyond* the Bible?

(pause to reflect)

As we have noted, the interpretation of the Bible as a developing understanding of God's revelation is sometimes found *within* the

Bible. At other times it is found *within and beyond* the Bible. At still other times it is found *beyond* the Bible. Are you willing to consider these three distinctions as possibilities? Are you leaning toward making them a part of your outlook? Or have you already assimilated them into your understanding?

QUESTIONS

1. *How would you explain the difference between a static and an unfolding expression of God's revelation?*

2. *Do you interpret the Bible as a static expression or a developing understanding of God's revelation? Can you give some examples to illustrate what you mean?*

3. *What difference does it make if an individual uses one approach or the other?*

4. *How do you understand the distinctions between within the Bible, within and beyond the Bible, and beyond the Bible?*

5. *Do you find these distinctions helpful? valid? essential?*

6. *On the basis of your reflections and your interactions with others, is it time to stop interpreting the Bible in a static rather than a developing understanding of God's revelation? What do you think?*

Is it time to stop calling homosexuality a sin without clarifying what we mean?

Maybe yes. Maybe no. What do you think?

I met Robert Traina when I was a seminary student at The Biblical Seminary in New York (now New York Theological Seminary). He was the embodiment of the institution, known for his passionate commitment to the Bible and his teaching of an inductive method of studying the Bible. His book, *Methodical Bible Study* (1952), sets forth his approach in four overall steps: Observation, Interpretation, Evaluation and Application, and Correlation.

I served as Dr. Traina's graduate assistant for three years while in New York, and maintained my relationship with him for subsequent years, even after he moved to Kentucky to become dean of Asbury Theological Seminary. While there, he joined with David Bauer and published a further development of his approach in the book, *Inductive Bible Study: A Comprehensive Guide to the Practice of Hermeneutics* (2011).

Two of the most important contributions this methodology made to my understanding of the Bible are: (1) the contextual interpretation of particular passages and (2) the evaluation of those passages. The first one is a process that attempts to determine the meaning of a small unit of the biblical text—a word, a phase, a sentence, or a brief paragraph—in light of its location in a part of the book, and then in the book itself. This focus on context is an attempt to avoid *proof texting*—an interpretation that takes a small unit out of its surrounding verses and chapters.

The second one is a process to determine whether the meaning of a passage is local and temporal, or universal and timeless. My own wording over the years has been the distinction between *cultural* and *transcultural* understanding. For example, one—among many I might identify—speaks of the necessity of women covering their heads with a veil and the requirement for men not to wear their hair long (1 Corinthians 11:2-16). Are these admonitions local or universal (cultural or transcultural)?

These methodological steps are essential, from my point of view, to include in the study of any biblical passage. Are they essential for you?

(pause to reflect)

This approach involves an awareness of both the literary context of a passage, as well as the historical situation out of which it emerges, and the primary audience to whom it is addressed. We will use it in developing an understanding of selected passages from the Pentateuch (Genesis 19:1-11; Leviticus 18:6-30 and 20:10-16) and from Paul (Romans 1:24-27 and 1 Corinthians 6:9-11) or written in Paul's name after his death (1 Timothy 1:9-10)—incidental passages that pertain to the subject of homosexuality. No passage discusses homosexual behavior in an extensive manner. Furthermore, of the 31,102 verses in the Bible, only about 100 verses embedded in a very select group of passages make a reference to some type of same-sex behavior. This means that 99.99 percent of the Bible doesn't even mention such behaviors.

Genesis 19 tells the story of what took place in the city of Sodom when Lot invited two angels disguised as men to spend the night in his home. A group of ruffians from the city, learning about Lot's visitors, came to his door, wanting to have sex with them. Lot refused to let them in, or let the men out, and offered the men his virgin daughters—clearly not a moral example to follow—in place of the men. They said no, they wanted the men so they could rape them (and thereby humiliate them). However, they were unsuccessful, and the visitors emerged unharmed when the attackers' eyes were blinded.

In the evaluation of this story (and perhaps Judges 19 which is a similar story), is there a universal or transcultural truth about homosexuality? Does it say anything about consensual activity between persons of the same sex? Or is it a story about evil men seeking to demean and disgrace guests who are passing through a city?

It's interesting that the word *sodomy,* which refers to the coercive homosexual acts a group of men from the city of Sodom wanted to carry out, has broadened its connotation to encompass a variety of exploitive sexual activities. However, for some biblical writers (e.g., Ezekiel) the people of Sodom lived with "pride, excess of food, and prosperous case, but did not aid the poor and needy" (16:49). This failure to practice hospitality seems to have been the primary issue that identified the people of Sodom, not the issue of homosexual behavior. (See also the interpretation of Sodom by Jesus in chapter 9.)

Leviticus 18:6-30 addresses the men of Israel and includes these words: "You shall not lie with a male as with a woman" (verse 22). Likewise, Leviticus 20:1-27 expresses the same thought, though this time it is addressed to all the people of Israel.

These verses identify one prohibition in the midst of a series of others that begin with the words: "None of you shall approach anyone near of kin to uncover nakedness" (18:6), a reference to the genitals of another person, seen with the eyes, and perhaps responded to sexually. A list follows (18:7-23) that includes the following women: mother, father's wife, sister, father's daughter, mother's daughter, son's daughter, daughter's daughter, father's wife's daughter, father's sister, mother's sister, father's brother's wife, daughter-in-law, brother's wife, woman and her daughter, her son's daughter, her daughter's daughter, woman as a rival to your sister, woman in her menstrual uncleanness, and kinsman's wife. Then, as if this wasn't inclusive enough, the writer goes on to state three other prohibitions in this discussion of incest, one of which is: "You shall not lie with a male as with a woman; it is an abomination" (18:22).

This particular prohibition is set in the context of a patriarchal culture in which men were thought to be superior and therefore dominant over women. For men to play the role of women was considered an insult, a disgrace, and an abomination. In addition, this prohibition and all the others in this chapter are descriptions of episodic events to be avoided in order to maintain the purity of the people of Israel.

These verses in Leviticus 18 and 20 appear in a section of Leviticus commonly known as the Holiness Code (chapters 17–26). In this part of the book, the Israelites are admonished to preserve their identity as the people of God, set apart from the practices of other people around them. God speaks to Moses and says: "You shall not do as they do in the land of Egypt, where you lived, and you shall not do as they do in the land of Canaan, to which I am bringing you" (18:3). In other words, the writer is addressing a local situation that is referring to cultic fertility practices, rather than a universal understanding that sets forth a timeless appropriation. Was the writer expressing his visceral response to cultural abominations in this setting, as other writers did in their circumstances (e.g., the writer of 1 Kings 14:24, when he speaks of "male temple prostitutes" committing the abominations of the nations)?

(pause to reflect)

Many laws in Leviticus are negative, explaining what should not be done (e.g., in 11:2-47 and other passages): eating shellfish such as shrimp, insects, birds, and animals of various kinds; wearing two types of fabric; sowing two kinds of seed in the same field; tattooing; etc. However, some laws are positive, expressing what should be done (e.g., in 19:18—loving your neighbor as yourself). Was the writer in this particular verse setting forth a universal or transcultural understanding when he identified such an expression of love, rather than referring to a way of life that was only meant to be local and temporal?

Passages related to same-sex behavior are also few and far between in the New Testament. Hebrew has no word that is equivalent to our English word *homosexual*; neither does Greek. In the 1946 New Testament edition of the Revised Standard Version, *homosexual* was used to translate two words, *malakos* and *arsenokoites*, as if they were one word in 1 Corinthians 6:9. However, realizing that such a translation was inaccurate—drawing a conclusion not warranted by the Greek text—the translation committee dropped *homosexual* and replaced it with *sexual perverts* in its next edition in 1971. The use of the word *homosexual* in this and other passages in the New Testament is not a precise rendering of any Greek word. Translations that use it are reading a point of view into the text that is not explicitly there—what scholars call *eisegesis* (reading meaning *into* the text) rather than *exegesis* (reading meaning *out of* the text).

Several nonbiblical authors in the first century—Seneca, Plutarch, Dio Chrysostom, Philo, and others—describe various beliefs and practices of Greco-Roman culture. Included as a part of these experiences of same-sex behavior are: (1) sex between adult men and young boys or older youth, (2) male prostitution, (3) sex between masters and slaves, (4) rape, and (5) promiscuous sexual episodes. All of these were rampant in that society, especially in large urban areas such as Corinth and Rome.

According to those ancient writers, one of the more common practices was sex between men and boys or youth. It is called *pederasty*, and the adult man is known as a *pederast*. Sometimes these encounters involved a coming of age ritual; at other times they were for pleasure. On occasion, money or other favors were given. Coercion was not uncommon, particularly when the boy or youth was a slave or the son of a slave. Such practices—widespread in the world of the first century—represent behaviors that are unacceptable to us today.

(pause to reflect)

Of the three New Testament passages related to same-sex behavior, we find the earliest (written in the 50s of the first century) in 1 Corinthians 6:9-10: "Do you not know that wrongdoers will not inherit the kingdom of God? Do not be deceived! Fornicators, idolaters, adulterers, male prostitutes, sodomites, thieves, the greedy, drunkards, revilers, robbers—none of these will inherit the kingdom of God."

The context for Paul's understanding of same-sex behavior was the cultural perspective of the nonbiblical writers of his time. Even though he gives a list of wrongdoers that is broader in scope, he includes two words that the New Revised Standard Version (NRSV) translates as *male prostitutes* and *sodomites*. The Greek word for the former is *malakos*. Its root meaning (according to the dictionary that is a part of *The Greek New Testament* published by the United Bible Societies) is *soft*. The King James Version uses *effeminate*, which might be the closest English equivalent.

The Greek word for the other term is *arsenokoites*, a word that is not found anywhere in or beyond the Bible, except for one verse in First Corinthians and one verse in First Timothy. Its root meaning (according to the same dictionary) is *male sexual pervert*. Sometimes *malakos* is put together with *arsenokoites* and translated as *effeminate males* and *men who have sex with them*. That is one way of connecting the two words, though this borders on being an interpretation rather than a translation.

Sometimes these two Greek words in 1 Corinthians 6:9 are combined and translated—erroneously—as *men who have sex with men* (New International Version), or *both participants in same- sex intercourse* (Common English Bible). The *textual* footnote in the NIV also gives an incorrect interpretation by stating: "The words *men who have sex with men* translate two Greek words that refer to the passive and active participants in homosexual acts." The CEB also gives an incorrect *textual* footnote by adding the words "submissive and dominant male sexual partners." Neither of these two translations accurately represents what the Greek text says. Are they examples of reading an understanding *into* the text, rather than *out* of the text?

Moreover, is the entire catalog of vices in this passage applicable to a local situation? Or is the list itself local, except for the final universal conclusion (i.e., that these wrongdoers will not inherit the kingdom of God)?

Paul writes the Epistle of First Corinthians to a particular "church" in Corinth, one that had already written a letter to Paul, asking him a series of questions (beginning with 7:1). They had not asked anything about homosexuality, though they did ask about a particular heterosexual matter involving a man who was living with his father's wife (5:1-5).

When Paul was in Corinth, he wrote a letter to "all God's beloved in Rome" (Romans 1:7). He does not refer to them as a "church" as he does at the beginning of all his other epistles. Neither does he respond to their questions. Paul had never been to Rome when he wrote his letter to them.

In a lengthy and sophisticated theological analysis of sin, redemption, and other related matters, he includes the following passage in Romans 1:24-25: "Therefore God gave them up in the lusts of their hearts to impurity, to the degrading of their bodies among themselves, because they exchanged the truth about God for a lie and worshiped and served the creature rather than the Creator, who is blessed forever!" In these particular verses from Romans 1, his focus is on idolatry—their worship of the creature rather than the creator.

In the verses that follow—1:26-27—Paul expresses some of the symptoms that emerge when people live by such idolatry: "For this reason God gave them up to degrading passions. Their women exchanged natural intercourse for unnatural, and in the same way also the men, giving up natural intercourse with women, were consumed with passion for one another. Men committed shameless acts with men and received in their own persons the due penalty for their error." It is clear that God allowed those in Rome to follow their lusts and passions.

What is not so clear is who they were and what they were doing. Let's remember Paul had not met them, since he had not yet come to Rome. Let's also remember that Paul wrote epistles that interpreters call *occasional letters*. That is, he was addressing particular occasions that prompted his writing, even in his letter to the Romans (especially 15:22–16:27).

In verses 26 and 27 of chapter 1, Paul surmises that the women to which he refers exchanged what was natural intercourse (a woman and a man) for what was unnatural (presumably a woman and a woman). Likewise the men he identifies exchanged what was natural intercourse (a man and a woman) for what was unnatural (presumably a man and a man). Intercourse for the purpose of procreation was natural. It had always been understood that way.

Men in Rome—or at least those whom Paul was addressing—were consumed with passion for one another and committed shameless acts with other men. Were they engaged in typical sexual behavior that we have already discussed earlier in this chapter where we identified behaviors in five different categories? Were there also other encounters that Paul had in mind such as male temple prostitution or particular cultic rituals?

Whatever the circumstances, I think we can assume it was not same-sex behavior in a committed, long-term relationship. We don't have any evidence for such relationships in Romans or anywhere else in the New Testament. However, we do have evidence in these verses from Romans, and verses in other books, that there were episodic events that were promiscuous—some of which were certainly abusive and exploitive.

(pause to reflect)

In a brief list of vices in 1 Timothy 1:9-10—a letter that is Pauline in thought and tone, though it might have been written in Paul's name after his death—the writer includes words similar to those in First Corinthians: "This means understanding that the law is laid down not for the innocent but for the lawless and disobedient, for the godless and sinful, for the unholy and profane, for those who kill their father or mother, for murderers, fornicators, sodomites, slave traders, liars, perjurers, and whatever else is contrary to the sound teaching that conforms to the glorious gospel of the blessed God, which he entrusted to me." It is interesting that the

NRSV translates the word *pornos* as *fornicators* in this passage and 1 Corinthians 6:9, while it translates the same word in 1 Corinthians 5:9 as *sexually immoral persons.*

The word that follows fornicators is *arsenokoites,* a person who is a *male sexual pervert* (discussed earlier in this chapter). Sometimes this Greek word is translated—erroneously—as *those practicing homosexuality* (NIV), or *people who have intercourse with the same sex* (CEB). Both of these translations are not only incorrect, but they are misleading to the reader, since that wording is not in the Greek text. Is this another example of reading an interpretation *into* the text, rather than *out of* the text?

In this passage from First Timothy, and the passages cited from First Corinthians and Romans, the context for Paul (and the writer of First Timothy if it was not Paul) was the perspective of the first century. The names given to the behaviors reflected the cultural understanding of that time.

A few years ago I taught a six-week course at St. Luke's United Methodist Church in Indianapolis titled *The Other Gospels*—a topic requested by a number of members of the congregation. Since the series was open to the public, a few people from other churches came. One of those persons asked me a question in the middle of a session. "Dr. Hansen," he began, "do you take the Bible literally?"

I answered: "Yes"—paused for a couple of seconds, noting his smile, and the perplexed look on the faces of others in the class, and then said—"sometimes." I then cited a couple of examples where I took the Bible literally, a couple where I did not, and then suggested we talk further after class.

I've been thinking I might give a similar response if someone asked me: "Is the practice of homosexuality a sin?" I would probably respond by saying, "Yes, . . . sometimes."

And then if someone asked me, "Is the practice of heterosexuality a sin?" I would probably answer, "Yes, . . . sometimes."

(pause to reflect)

What I mean is that I believe some practices are sinful for homosexuals and for heterosexuals; some are not. When a man exploits another man, or a woman exploits another woman, it is sinful. When a man exploits a woman, or a woman exploits a man, it is sinful. Sin is sin, whether it is between two gay men, two lesbian women, or two heterosexual individuals.

Likewise, when a man carries on a promiscuous relationship with another man or a woman carries on a promiscuous relationship with another woman, it is sinful. When a man carries on a promiscuous relationship with a woman or a woman carries on a promiscuous relationship with a man, it is also sinful. Once again, sin is sin!

Is this the way you see it?

QUESTIONS

1. *Is it sufficient to repeat what the Bible says, or is it essential to discern what the Bible means?*

2. *Are the surrounding verses, paragraphs, and chapters in which a passage is found important to discern in order to avoid taking a verse out of context and thereby risking a misunderstanding of the passage?*

3. *Is the process of evaluation necessary to determine if a passage is local or universal—cultural or transcultural—in its meaning?*

4. *Are the Old and New Testament passages talking about homosexuality in a general sense? Or are they speaking about same-sex behavior in particular situations?*

5. *What do you think the Bible teaches about homosexuality? What biblical and historical evidence can you offer to substantiate your point of view?*

6. *On the basis of your reflections and your interaction with others, is it time to stop calling homosexuality a sin without clarifying what we mean? What do you think?*

Is it time to stop believing the Bible condemns a homosexual orientation without giving up the authority of the Bible?

Maybe yes. Maybe no. What do you think?

I continued to study with Robert Traina at The Biblical Seminary in New York while pursuing a second master's degree. My interest expanded beyond a methodical process of studying the Bible to an examination of the inspiration and authority of Scripture. In the second half of that year, I wrote a thesis titled *Issues Involved in the Inspiration of Scripture.*

During my high school and college years, I had become very interested in the Bible, studying it in formal as well as informal settings, participating in memorization programs, and reading it regularly for personal devotions. I tried to use it as my authority for what I thought and how I lived.

In that process I was taught that the Bible was inerrant in its original autographs. I accepted that point of view and even argued as persuasively as I could in defense of its claims. However, in carrying out research for my thesis, I encountered a question that would prove to be very problematical for me: Is inerrancy necessary for authority? I thought the answer was yes; but I discovered—over a period of months—that the copies of the Bible I was using day by day were not without any error.

My dilemma was this: either the Bible was not my authority, or inerrancy was not needed for authority. I spent many hours trying to work out an answer. I finally came to these conclusions: (1) that I didn't need inerrancy for authority, (2) that the copies I was reading and studying were my authority, and (3) that I needed to affirm that the Bible I used was trustworthy and reliable.

(pause to reflect)

Furthermore, I deeply appreciated the statement that "all scripture is inspired by God" (2 Timothy 3:16), even though I learned that the Greek word translated *scripture* was *writing*—a word that was also used as a general term in other noncanonical writings. I also learned that "all" was not a reference to the entire Bible, since the twenty-seven books in the New Testament were not identified as a collection until the year 367 CE, and the collection of books in the Old Testament had not yet been finalized. The reference was probably to the Septuagint, the Greek translation of the Old Testament, or at least those sections known as the Law and the Prophets.

Nevertheless, the affirmation in verse 16 that these writings are "inspired by God" and "useful for teaching, for reproof, for correction, and for training in righteousness," was encouraging and empowering. This affirmation, and the conclusions I stated earlier, became the basis for the authority of the Bible—in my life, and in the life of the church and the world. Furthermore, the authority of the Bible became the most central belief in all of my theology, not only in what I studied, but how I committed myself to live. I learned my life was the best translation of the Bible I could ever have!

Individuals talk about their view of Scripture in different ways. Some say they have a *true* view of Scripture. I wonder whether they mean that their personal view is the true one, and if you disagree with them, you are told—implicitly or explicitly—that your view is not true. Others say they have a *high* view of Scripture. I wonder whether they mean that their personal view is the high one, and if you disagree with them, you have a low view, or at least a lower one.

Still others say they have a *traditional* view of Scripture. I think less about what they mean since I claim at least one understanding of this view. As a United Methodist, I turn to how the church views the Bible. More specifically, I turn to the documents of the UMC and affirm what our documents say (¶104 in *The Book of Discipline 2016*).

First among them is *The Articles of Religion of The Methodist Church*. In Article V we have this statement:

> The Holy Scripture containeth all things necessary to salvation; so that whatsoever is not read therein, nor may be proved thereby, is not to be required of any man that it should be believed as an article of faith, or be thought requisite or necessary to salvation.

The second is *The Confession of Faith of the Evangelical United Brethren Church*. In Article IV we have this confession:

> We believe the Holy Bible, Old and New Testaments, reveals the Word of God so far as it is necessary for our salvation. It is to be received through the Holy Spirit as the true rule and guide for faith and practice. Whatever is not revealed in or

established by the Holy Scriptures is not to be made an article
of faith nor is it to be taught as essential to salvation.

The third is *The General Rules of the Methodist Church,* and
contains three parts (stated here in summary form):
First: doing no harm.
Second: doing good.
Third: attending upon all the ordinances of God.
>Public worship of God.
>Ministry of the Word, either read or expounded.
>Supper of the Lord.
>Family and private prayer.
>Searching the Scriptures.
>Fasting or abstinence.

These are the General Rules of our societies; all of which
we are taught of God to observe, even in his written Word,
which is the only rule, and the sufficient rule, both of our
faith and practice.

The United Methodist Hymnal includes a section entitled "Affirmations of Faith" (880–889). One of these, *The Nicene Creed* (which
comes from the Council of Constantinople in the year 381), has a
phrase, "in accordance with the Scriptures." It follows the phrase,
"On the third day he rose again"—a statement that does not deal
with a particular view of Scripture. *The Apostles' Creed* (both the
traditional version and the ecumenical version) does not have
any reference to the Bible—understandably since the list of twenty-seven books we have as our New Testament, did not surface
until the year 367 CE in a festal letter of Athanasius. Other creedal
statements in the hymnal that do not have any reference to the
Bible include: (1) *A Statement of Faith of the United Church of Can-*

ada, (2) *A Modern Affirmation,* and (3) *The World Methodist Social Affirmation.*

The creedal formulation that includes a reference to the Bible is the document titled *A Statement of Faith of the Korean Methodist Church.* It states: "We believe in the Word of God contained in the Old and New Testaments as the sufficient rule both of faith and of practice." This statement is similar to the wording in Article V of *The Articles of Religion of the Methodist Church,* and Article IV of *The Confession of Faith of the Evangelical United Brethren Church* (both already identified in this chapter).

Combining the wording of these three statements, we can define the *traditional* view of Scripture in The United Methodist Church in these words: *The Bible reveals the Word of God contained in the Old and New Testaments as the true and sufficient rule for both faith and practice.*

The *traditional* view of Scripture is my belief, as well as the basis for my commitment to Wesleyan vitality, biblical theology, and Holy Spirit empowerment. Is this also your view?

(pause to reflect)

In what way is the Bible our authority in matters of faith and practice? Is knowing what it says sufficient? Or is it also necessary to determine its meaning at the time it was written and then, through a process of evaluation, decide what it means today? As we carry out such a process, is it important to compare our conclusions with other biblical interpreters—those who agree with us and those who do not? Is it also important to search for evidence from a variety of sources, and then follow the evidence wherever it leads?

In my earlier years as a student of the Bible, I believed the Bible denounced everything that had to do with same-sex relationships. That's what I had been told—indirectly and directly—by my pastor, my youth leader, and my friends at church. I accepted it because all those around me believed it. I didn't think about other possibilities. And I wasn't aware of anyone who was gay or lesbian. (Keep in mind this was decades ago.)

I didn't try to understand what the Bible had to say on this subject since I didn't even know where to look in the Bible. However, as I went through my undergraduate and graduate education, I began to examine what the Bible said, and what the Bible meant, though I still approached the Bible with my mind made up—a close-minded approach I used on many different topics. As time went on, numerous questions arose in my thinking on the subject of homosexuality, as well as other subjects. I eventually learned to examine the biblical evidence, and follow wherever it led— even when that place was different from what I had believed. The Bible—not some interpretation of the Bible—became my authority in matters of belief (faith) and living (practice).

What has been your development in learning about what the Bible says and what the Bible means regarding same-sex orientation? Is it similar to my journey? or somewhat different?

(pause to reflect)

Over a number of decades of studying the Bible, I have come to the conclusion—slowly, yet deliberately—that the Bible does not say a *same-sex orientation* is wrong or evil and does not in any way denounce it. It simply does not address it (i.e., who a person wants to be with, is attracted to, and feels drawn to emotionally, romantically, and sexually someone of the same sex). It is an understanding of our generation—one that was not a part of the culture at the time in which the Bible was written.

Furthermore, The United Methodist Church does not denounce a person with such an orientation either. As we noted in chapter 1, the Judicial Council, in speaking about the ordained ministry in Decision 1027, says: "No provision of the *Discipline* bars a person with a same-sex orientation from the ordained ministry of The United Methodist Church."

On the basis of a lack of condemnation in the Bible regarding persons with a same-sex orientation, and an approval of these persons for ordination, is it time to accept, rather than condemn, persons who have a same-sex orientation?

QUESTIONS

1. *Do you believe in the authority of the Bible? If so, what do you mean when you say this?*

2. *What is your understanding of a traditional view of Scripture? Do you agree with this view?*

3. *In what ways is the Bible your authority in matters of faith and practice?*

4. *What does it mean when someone says the Bible does not condemn a same-sex orientation? Do you agree with that statement?*

5. *How do you understand the sentence included in Decision 1027 of the Judicial Council? Do you agree with it?*

6. *On the basis of your own reflections and your interaction with others, is it time to stop believing the Bible condemns a homosexual orientation without giving up the authority of the Bible? What do you think?*

Is it time to stop asserting that Jesus' view of homosexuality is the same as ours?

Maybe yes. Maybe no. What do you think?

I interviewed faculty members at three leading universities when I was thinking of pursuing a doctoral program in Early Christianity—a common approach when a multi year commitment is staring you in the face. One of these persons was Ernest Saunders, a faculty member at Northwestern University and Garrett Theological Seminary. He, more than anyone else I met, exemplified all the essential qualities I was seeking in a doctoral adviser.

A critical principle I learned from him was his gracious insistence that I thoroughly examine all relevant evidence in my research and then follow the evidence to whatever conclusion it would lead. This meant an honest recognition of my assumptions and biases, and a willingness to set one or more of them aside and change my interpretation if the evidence warranted it.

Sometime during my first year of study, we were examining the narrative of John 13:1-20, where the writer tells the story of Jesus washing the disciples' feet. It led me to remember a lengthy paper I had written while a seminary student a few years earlier, in which I attempted to show that the last few days of Jesus' life—described in all four Gospels—could be integrated into one consistent sequence of events. I had felt a need to do this because I had an assumption that it all had to fit together in one consistent story.

However, during the time I wrote that paper, I felt uncomfortable with the way I was interpreting certain verses in John to make it turn out that way. I shared this attempt, and the discomfort I sensed with Dr. Saunders, who simply said, "Perhaps you'll find it helpful if you review those passages in John, as well as the Synoptic Gospels." I indicated I would do that and let him know my results. And then, as I left his office, I remembered his words: "Follow the evidence wherever it leads."

With this principle in mind, I was ready to review the passages in John and compare them with those in the Synoptic Gospels. The first passage I examined began with the words: "Now before the Festival of the Passover," implying that this event took place before the celebration of Passover (13:1). The text goes on to say: "And during supper, Jesus . . . got up from the table . . . and began to wash the disciples' feet" (13:2-5). If this is the time indicator, would this mean that the washing of the disciples' feet took place at an evening meal that was the day before the Passover meal?

Luke, on the other hand, has Jesus saying to his disciples: "I have eagerly desired to eat this Passover with you before I suffer" (22:15). Is this a different understanding of the evening meal set forth by John?

Following the story of Jesus washing the feet of the disciples, and an extensive section of Jesus teaching (14:1–17:26), John says: "Then they took Jesus from Caiaphas to Pilate's headquarters. It was early in the morning. They themselves did not enter the headquarters, so as to avoid ritual defilement and to be able to eat the Passover" (18:28). Did this mean the Passover had not yet occurred? Furthermore, John explains: "When Pilate heard these words, he brought Jesus outside and seated him on the judge's bench. . . . Now it was the day of Preparation for the Passover; and it was about noon" (19:13-14).

Does the evidence in these passages in John lead to these conclusions: (1) that John sets forth a different chronology than the Synoptic Gospels? (2) that John has Jesus' death taking place at the same time as the lambs were being slain for the Passover meal? (3) that the Passover was celebrated after Jesus died? Do these conclusions also help us understand why John—at the beginning of his Gospel—declares: "Here is the Lamb of God who takes away the sin of the world" (1:29)?

(pause to reflect)

I have gone into this much detail to illustrate the principle of *following the evidence wherever it leads*, even if the conclusion does not fit the assumption that might have been held before the study was carried out. It is this principle I have sought to follow in the preceding chapters of this book and in this chapter.

Is it time to stop asserting that Jesus' view of homosexuality is the same as ours—the same as mine or the same as yours? I might assume that Jesus' view and my view were the same, even without consciously realizing it. You might do the same, even if our individual views were different from each other. Making such an assumption might lead me—might lead you—to feel comfortable. On the other hand, each of us might feel uncomfortable if we thought our individual perspectives were not the same as that which Jesus held. What thoughts come to mind, and what feelings surface, as you reflect on the assumptions you are making?

(pause to reflect)

On the basis of what Jesus says in all his statements in the Gospels, I think we can draw a firm conclusion, namely, that Jesus did not say anything about the subject of homosexuality. Therefore, whatever assumptions we make about Jesus' view, and our views on this subject, we need to be careful not to read into his statements what we want him to say.

However, Jesus did speak about some related matters. One of these is his discussion of marriage as it relates to the resurrection. All three Synoptic Gospels (Mark 12:18-27; Luke 20:27-40; Matthew 22:23-33) speak about a dispute the Sadducees were having.

Another is Jesus' discussion regarding divorce and its relationship to marriage—also included in each of the first three Gospels (Mark 10:1-12; Luke 16:18; Matthew 5:31-32, and 19:1-12). The similarities and differences in these texts become clear by using a volume such as the New Revised Standard Version of *Gospel Parallels: A Comparison of the Synoptic Gospels*, edited by Burton H. Throckmorton (Thomas Nelson, 1992). Or you might use a volume that contains all four Gospels such as the Common English Bible version of *Gospel Parallels*, edited by Joel B. Green and W. Gil Shin (Common English Bible, 2012). Or, if you read Greek, you might use the *Synopsis Quattuor Evangeliorum*, edited by Kurt Aland (Württembergischen Bibelanstalt Stuttgart, 1964). Using one of these sources will enable you—as it does me—to note more easily the variations between the Gospels. (This is what I did at the beginning of this chapter when I compared the passages dealing with the last days of the life of Jesus.)

In the narrative dealing with marriage and the resurrection, the variations are insignificant. However, in the discussion of marriage and divorce, there is a significant variation. Mark 10:1-12 (written in the late 60s of the first century) records the following teaching:

> He left that place and went to the region of Judea and beyond the Jordan. And crowds again gathered around him; and, as was his custom, he again taught them.
>
> Some Pharisees came, and to test him they asked, "Is it lawful for a man to divorce his wife?" He answered them, "What did Moses command you?" They said, "Moses allowed a man to write a certificate of dismissal and to divorce her." But Jesus said to them, "Because of your hardness of heart he wrote this commandment for you. But from the beginning of creation, 'God made them male and female.' 'For this reason a man shall leave his father and mother and be joined to his wife, and the two shall become one flesh.' So they are no longer two, but one flesh. Therefore what God has joined together, let no one separate."
>
> Then in the house the disciples asked him again about this matter. He said to them, "Whoever divorces his wife and marries another commits adultery against her; and if she divorces her husband and marries another, she commits adultery."

Jesus speaks about the central teaching regarding divorce when he says: "Whoever divorces his wife and marries another commits adultery against her; and if she divorces her husband and marries another, she commits adultery" (10:11-12). No exception is given; it's a categorical statement!

Luke (written in the mid 80s, with Mark as one of his sources) records the same teaching, though he gives a shortened version, one that focuses only on the man: "Anyone who divorces his wife and marries another commits adultery, and whoever marries a woman divorced from her husband commits adultery" (16:18). Again, no exception is made.

A different perspective is given in Matthew 19:1-12 (written in the mid 80s, with Mark as one of his sources) and an additional statement in 5:31-32. Jesus speaks about divorce, and according to Matthew, says: "Whoever divorces his wife, except for unchastity, and marries another commits adultery" (19:9). This exception is not found in Mark or in Luke. Did Jesus actually say it? Not according to Mark, who wrote his Gospel almost twenty years earlier than Matthew; and not according to Luke.

When you consider the evidence regarding whether Jesus made this exception, what do you conclude? It's not an easy task. Did Jesus say them both at different times? Did he change his mind? Or do you come to the conclusion to which I have come, namely, that Mark and Luke probably have the actual words of Jesus, while Matthew probably modified the teaching in light of the audience he was trying to reach in the 80s. The question Matthew raises in verse 3, "Is it lawful for a man to divorce his wife for any cause?" gives him the opportunity to provide an answer.

You might find it helpful to keep in mind that multiple rabbinical schools existed in the 80s—and earlier—groups that debated what the acceptable causes for divorce might be. In light of those discussions, the statement in Matthew's version would represent the strictest and most limited exception among the options that surfaced in these ongoing debates.

Earlier in this book, we differentiated between a developing understanding of God's revelation *within* the Bible, *within and beyond* the Bible and *beyond* the Bible (chapter 6). In that discussion we mentioned *divorce* as an example of the developing understanding of God's revelation *beyond* the Bible. However, we did not indicate that changes in society influenced the UMC and other denominations to accept divorce for a variety of reasons, even allowing *no fault* divorce to emerge. As mentioned in chapter 6, today laypersons, as well as clergy—even denominational executives, district superintendents, and bishops—become divorced, and no one is excluded from ministry because of this status.

Isn't this a considerable change—even a dramatic one—from what Jesus said according to Mark and Luke, and even from the one exception included in Jesus' statement in Matthew's passages?

(pause to reflect)

Since The United Methodist Church and other judicatories have accepted divorce as part of the developing understanding of God's revelation *beyond* the Bible—on the basis of changes within society—is it time for the UMC to accept a developing understanding of God's revelation regarding committed, long-term relationships of two people of the same sex? What do you think? Is saying no consistent with how we view divorce—a way of life that neglects and even goes directly against what Jesus taught?

Does our understanding of divorce, and our understanding of long-term monogamous relationships of same-sex couples, need to be integrated into our comprehension of the unfolding expression of God's revelation?

Jesus also has something to say about marriage and adultery. In the passage from Mark 10:1-12 (already cited), Jesus says: "God made them male and female," insisting on the equality in marriage intended in the Creation stories, rather than the Pharisees' focus on divorce as a male prerogative. Jesus then goes on to explain: "For this reason a man shall leave his father and mother and be joined to his wife, and the two shall become one flesh"—an affirmation of procreation as the primary function of marriage. And then he adds these words: "What God has joined together, let no one separate"—a strong admonition against divorce.

It's difficult—perhaps even unwise—to compare other dimensions of marriage, since the meaning of marriage developed over time *within* the Bible (as discussed in chapter 6), and developed within civilizations of the world over many centuries. What those of us who live in the United States understand the meaning of marriage to be—including the distinction between a legal document and a covenantal agreement—is neither the same as it once was, nor what it might become—not only in this country, but also in other countries of the world. Laws develop, and laws change. Applications of laws unfold, and applications of laws change.

One additional teaching from Jesus that relates to homosexuality is his reference to Sodom and Gomorrah in his discussion of the sending out of the twelve (Matthew 9:38–10:16). In verses 14 and 15, Jesus says: "If anyone will not welcome you or listen to your words, shake off the dust from your feet as you leave that house or town. Truly I tell you, it will be more tolerable for the land of Sodom and Gomorrah on the day of judgment than for that town."

Do you agree that the dominant sin of these cities that Jesus is addressing is not homosexuality (as we already discussed in chapter 7), but the lack of hospitality—the unwillingness to welcome the stranger?

Trying to understand the depth of sin that evoked strong feelings and thoughts from Jesus is not difficult if we conscientiously seek to comprehend what bothered him the most. Examining just one passage among many—the self-righteousness and hypocrisy of the religious leaders in Matthew 23—gives us a glimpse of what really concerned Jesus. Does this passage, and many others like them, contain messages for religious leaders of our day—for you and for me? If so, what would those messages be?

(pause to reflect)

Attempting to grasp the dimensions of love that opened up the heart, soul, mind, and strength of Jesus is made clear in many of his works and deeds. One example is his sharing these words from the depth of his being: "Just as I have loved you, you also should love one another. By this everyone will know that you are my disciples, if you have love for one another" (John 13:34-35). Is this more important—for Jesus and for us—than any of the views we hold regarding homosexuality?

When I was fourteen years old, a friend of our family gave my parents the book by Charles M. Sheldon, *In His Steps*—a book that focused on the question, What would Jesus do? Since my parents were immigrants who couldn't read English very well, they gave the book to me. I read it; I reflected on it over and over again; and I sought to integrate this question into many areas of my life— sometimes successfully, sometimes not.

Variations of that title have become central in my reflections about homosexuality:

- What would Jesus say?
- How would he say it?
- Why would he say it?

If the *historical Jesus* were here today, what would he say to leaders of Good News Movement, Reconciling Churches Network, Confessing Movement, Love Prevails, Wesleyan Covenant Association, Methodist Federation for Social Action, and all other United Methodist groups and local congregations in this country, and in all locations of United Methodist presence in the world?

And since the *risen Christ* is here today, what is he saying to the leaders of each of these groups?

QUESTIONS

1. *How would you explain to someone—a colleague, a family member, a friend—what it means "to follow the evidence wherever it leads" when studying the Bible?*

2. *Have you already been using this approach? In what additional ways—if any—would you want to develop it further?*

3. *In your understanding of the Bible, did Jesus have anything specific to say about homosexuality?*

4. *Are changes in the way we interpret divorce—even changes that clearly disagree with what Jesus said—an expression of the developing understanding of God's revelation beyond the Bible?*

5. *Are changes in the way we interpret homosexuality—changes that do not conflict with what Jesus said—an expression of the developing understanding of God's revelation beyond the Bible?*

6. *On the basis of your reflections and your interactions with others, is it time to stop asserting that Jesus' view of homosexuality is the same as ours? What do you think?*

Is it time to stop saying the practice of homosexuality is "incompatible with Christian teaching"?

Maybe yes. Maybe no. What do you think?

The meeting took place in Atlanta in the spring of 1972. This was the first time The United Methodist Church—the newly merged Methodist Church and Evangelical United Brethren Church—held a General Conference.

One of the items on the agenda was a proposal from the Social Principles Study Commission that had been created at the 1968 General Conference. One of the sections in that report was called "Human Sexuality." It stated the following:

> We recognize that sexuality is a good gift of God, and we believe persons may be fully human only when that gift is acknowledged and affirmed by themselves, the church, and society. We call all persons to disciplines that lead to the fulfillment of themselves, others, and society in the stewardship of this gift. Medical, theological, and humanistic

disciplines should combine in a determined effort to understand human sexuality more completely.

Although men and women are sexual beings whether or not they are married, sex between a man and a woman is to be clearly affirmed only in the marriage bond. Sex may become exploitive within as well as outside marriage. We reject all sexual expressions which damage or destroy the humanity God has given us as birthright, and we affirm only that sexual expression which enhances that same humanity, in the midst of diverse opinion as to what constitutes that enhancement. Homosexuals no less than heterosexuals are persons of sacred worth, who need the ministry and guidance of the church in their struggles for human fulfillment, as well as the spiritual and emotional care of a fellowship which enables reconciling relationships with God, with others, and with self. Further we insist that all persons are entitled to have their human and civil rights ensured.

A delegate on the floor made a motion that recommended the replacement of the final period with a comma, followed by these words: "although we do not condone the practice of homosexuality and consider this practice incompatible with Christian doctrine." After an amendment replaced the word "doctrine" with "teaching," the motion passed.

It is important to note that this amendment did not come through a study group, or any subgroup of the study commission itself. It was simply one delegate's motion. Following its adoption—especially in the weeks and months after General Conference was over—certain issues began to emerge.

One of the issues to arise early in that process was the lack of a definition of the word *homosexuality*—a complex term that the UMC has not yet clearly defined. (See chapter 1 for an overview of this matter.) A second issue that delegates did not thoroughly examine before approving the amendment was the relationship between *attraction* and *behavior*. (See chapter 2 for an analysis of this distinction.)

Two other undefined words in the motion were *Christian* and *teaching*. The former did not distinguish between what is, and is not, *Christian* about homosexuality. The latter did not indicate what the teaching is, or where to find it.

Furthermore, the word *incompatible* was not clarified in terms of its contradictory dimensions or its antagonistic relationships. In addition, no context was provided for what constitutes the incompatibility.

Following the general statement on this matter in 1972, the General Conference, with clarification by the Judicial Council, added the word *self-avowed* in the section in the *Book of Discipline* that deals with *The Ministry of the Ordained*, indicating that it applied to the certification, ordination, and appointment of ministers (¶304.3). In addition, *chargeable offenses* could be made against those who did not comply with this requirement (¶2702.1).

Furthermore, United Methodist clergy could not conduct ceremonies that celebrate homosexual unions, including but not limited to same-sex weddings, and these ceremonies could not take place in United Methodist churches (¶341.6, 2702.1). Clergy who did not comply with this requirement could face *charges*.

On the basis of these considerations, and others not yet included, is it time to stop saying the practice of homosexuality is "incompatible with Christian teaching"?

Before we draw firm conclusions regarding whether we say yes or no, let's look more precisely at five words: *Christian, teaching, incompatible, practicing,* and *self-avowed*.

First, it is interesting that the incompatibility is not with the Bible. At least the statement doesn't say that. Some persons talk about the practice of homosexuality, or homosexuality itself, being incompatible with the Bible. However, did the motion that was passed in 1972, or actions taken by subsequent General Conferences, say that?

(pause to reflect)

Others refer to the incompatibility with what is distinctly Christian. However, in what ways do these persons define or not define what they mean by *Christian*? Does it include any Christian expression: Protestant, Roman Catholic, Orthodox, etc.? Or, is it only a certain Christian group, for example, United Methodist?

Still others seem to make assumptions that indicate, or at least imply, there is clarity of Christian teaching to which they can appeal. Where would that teaching be found and what would it say? Do *The Articles of Religion of The Methodist Church*, or *The Confession of Faith of The Evangelical United Brethren Church*, or *The General Rules of The Methodist Church* make any reference to homosexuality? (See ¶104 in the *Book of Discipline* for these documents.) In addition, do any of the affirmations of faith in *The United Methodist Hymnal* (pages 880–889: *Nicene Creed, Apostles' Creed, Statement of Faith of the United Church of Canada, Statement of Faith of the Korean Methodist Church, Modern Affirmation, World Methodist Social Affirmation*, or the affirmations from selected biblical passages) make any reference to homosexuality?

(pause to reflect)

The word *practicing* was included in the statement of human sexuality that was affirmed in 1972. However, some people forget that modifier, or neglect to include it, and simply refer to homosexuality in an overall manner. There is a significant difference between an attraction to a person of the same sex and behavior based on that desire. (See chapter 2 for a more detailed discussion.)

In addition to the initial statement of 1972, the word *self-avowed* was added to *practicing homosexuals*. What these words mean has varied in individual situations and has led the Judicial Council over a period of three decades to make a number of decisions to clarify the meaning of the words and their application to particular situations (702, 708, 722, 725, 764, 844, 984, 985, 1020, 1027, and 1028). The most recent deliberations regarding the meaning of the words *self-avowed* occurred in 2017, when the Judicial Council stated: "A same-sex marriage license issued by competent civil authorities together with the clergyperson's status in a same-sex relationship is a public declaration that the person is a self-avowed practicing homosexual for purposes of ¶304.3 and ¶2702.1 (b)."

Inquiring into someone's personal life, especially in regard to one's sexual behavior, is considered by many to be inappropriate. Do you agree? Or disagree? If you are a heterosexual individual, how would you feel if you were pursuing a call to licensed or ordained ministry and were asked about your sexual behavior, not only by another individual but also by a person in authority—a local church representative, a district committee member, or one or more members of the Board of Ordained Ministry?

(pause to reflect)

Do you agree that those of us who are a part of The United Methodist Church have come to the point where we need to ask the question as to whether it is time to stop saying the practice of homosexuality is "incompatible with Christian teaching"? Furthermore, do you agree that we need to discuss our responses with one another in an attitude of openness to each other and an openness to the leading of the Holy Spirit?

QUESTIONS

1. At what point in time did you become aware of the prominence of the issue of homosexuality in The United Methodist Church? 1972? the 80s? the 90s? the 2000s?

2. How did the awareness emerge? Who told you about it? What did they say?

3. When did you begin to understand that there were different points of view on this subject?

4. With whom did you discuss this understanding? Did your conversations include persons with views other than your own?

5. What has emerged as your understanding of the statement in our Book of Discipline that says the practice of homosexuality is "incompatible with Christian teaching"? In what ways do you agree or disagree with what it says?

6. On the basis of your own reflections and your interactions with others, is it time to stop saying the practice of homosexuality is "incompatible with Christian teaching"? What do you think?

Part Three

Relational and Practical

Chapters 11–12

Is it time to stop fearing persons who have a sexual orientation or gender identity different from our own?

Maybe yes. Maybe no. What do you think?

It was a beautiful spring day as I drove up the winding driveway and parked my car outside the house. Before I could get out of the car, there she stood, with a gracious smile lighting up her face and a warm welcome in her outstretched arms—my mother whom I hadn't seen for months.

She was living by herself in a log cabin on a rural hillside in New Fairfield, Connecticut—originally a summer cabin, but now a winterized home. I had just flown in from Indianapolis to spend some time with her.

After swapping family news, my mother shared with me that she had new neighbors in the house closest to her—about fifty yards away. She indicated she didn't know much about the two men who had purchased and remodeled the house, but was glad to have someone nearby.

I spent my childhood summers in that log cabin and got to

know all the families on Rocky Hill Road. When newcomers moved in—which was not often—we would visit them and extend our hospitality. Therefore, it was not unusual for me to suggest to my mother that I would stop by and introduce myself to her neighbors since I had not yet met them.

Later that day I did walk over and visit the men. I welcomed them to the neighborhood and said I was glad they were there, especially since my eighty-five-year-old mother, living by herself, might need their assistance at some point. They expressed their willingness very generously and gave me their phone number.

When I returned to my mother's home, I told her about my visit. And then she surprised me with her comment: "They're fags, aren't they?" I replied I thought that was accurate that they are a couple, but I explained to her that we no longer use that word to refer to gay men. She quietly responded: "I'm so sorry. That's the only word I've ever heard." My mother was an immigrant from Norway who came to this country unable to speak English. But she was the most thoughtful and gracious individual I'd ever known.

After I explained some of my understanding of gay men, she thanked me. And then she said: "I knew they were different, but last Christmas, just after they had moved in, I brought them a container filled with homemade Norwegian cookies, cakes, and candy. They're my neighbors. As you know, I always love my neighbors—whoever they are." Tears welled up in my eyes and I hugged my mother and thanked her for being such a good neighbor.

How we respond to people who are different from us sometimes begins with kindness and generosity, though sometimes with apprehension—even fear—especially if we know very little about them. Words have developed in some circumstances to describe that sentiment. That's how the word *homophobia* surfaced in the

1960s. It's a combination of two Greek words, *homo* which means *same*, and *phobos* which means *fear*. In English usage, a *phobia* is an exaggerated and often inexplicable fear. When that meaning is connected with homosexuality, it refers to an irrational fear that can lead to an aversion, a prejudice, or even a discrimination against homosexual individuals.

One reason fear surfaces in this context is the attitude many of us have toward *change*. Much in our world is changing, and these developments often take place rapidly. In addition, they can be multiple in number, frequent in timing, and consequential in effect. And, as if this isn't enough, they can come to us vigorously and persistently, and many times can't be avoided. As we watch TV, or engage in various forms of social and print media, there seems to be no escape. As a result, our anxiety levels rise, and our feelings of fear escalate. In what ways is change a part of your experience?

A second reason fear emerges toward persons who have a sexual orientation or gender identity different from our own is fear of the unknown. What we don't know sometimes threatens us. At a deeper level, what we don't understand leads us to react in ways that might be uncomfortable for us, and confusing to others. It's easier to pretend that we know than to admit our ignorance and our lack of understanding. Furthermore, when our comprehension is limited, or simply wrong, we might draw inappropriate conclusions. If we are not corrected, or at least shown another point of view, we might become entrenched in an erroneous understanding, repeat that viewpoint over and over again, become close-minded, and end up unwilling to consider other perspectives. Following that pattern sometimes leads to fear, defensiveness, and anger that prevent open communication. Do you concur with this analysis?

A third reason is the sense of loss that sometimes springs up. For some it's the loss of a traditional understanding of the family—

the inclusion of persons who have a different sexual orientation or gender identity and the relationships that emerge among those persons. For others it's the loss of a personal culture—the invasion of others who have not been invited encroaching an individual's space. For still others, it seems like a movement down a slippery slope toward moral relativism. And for some of these persons, it seems like a loss of biblical authority (i.e., the way a certain interpretation of the Bible had been stated, over and over again). Have you experienced any of these losses?

A fourth reason involves feelings in addition to fear—feelings that sometimes intensify and even exaggerate fear. Uncertainty might create ambiguity and confusion and result in discomfort and uneasiness. Insecurity might lead to hesitancy, self-doubt, and vacillation. As a result, it might be natural to withdraw from engagement and build a wall for protection. Are one or more of these feelings part of your life?

(pause to reflect)

Before we identify what—hopefully—will be helpful ways to stop fearing persons who have a sexual orientation or gender identity different from our own, we need to remind ourselves that those persons might fear us—particularly if we are heterosexuals who are unfriendly to them. Those who are in a minority position—whatever that might be—often fear others who are in a majority position. Such fear, however, will probably not focus on fear of change, since LGBTQ individuals are a part of the change. Neither will it be directed to what is unknown, for they are significantly more aware of matters pertaining to sexual orientation and gender identity. Nor will it consider losses as highly significant since they will experience fewer of the losses we have identified.

Fear and related feelings often run deep within LGBTQ persons. At the core is the sense of uncertainty. It permeates their lives in numerous ways: how heterosexual individuals whom they haven't met, or don't really know, will react to them; how welcoming, passive, or hostile new situations will treat them; how dependable circumstances that have been accepting and affirming in the past will be in the present and the future.

(pause to reflect)

Sentiments like these often lead LGBTQ persons to experience discomfort and uneasiness. Relationships—so important in life—become ambiguous, even tenuous. Trust is threatened, sometimes weakened or even destroyed. And insecurity sometimes increases, rather than decreases, making it difficult and frustrating to keep explaining—over and over again—what heterosexuals don't seem to understand. And perhaps hardest of all, is the sharing of incredible struggles and pain, anguish and hurt, anger and abuse—experiences we will identify more fully in the next chapter.

I believe acknowledging fear is the most important starting point for all of us. For unacknowledged fear is often more powerful and destructive. It can surface—in countless ways—and can cause heartache and pain—sometimes without an individual realizing what is taking place.

For many people, acknowledging fear is difficult, because it includes the expression of feelings as well as the speaking of words. Giving a cognitive expression to an emotional sentiment simply does not work. Using words that come out of one's head is necessary, but insufficient. Sharing what lies deep within—what some call *vomiting our guts*—might be necessary for those persons whose words are sometimes filled with deep-seated negative feelings. Such emotional sharing is essential and can be wholesome if feelings are expressed in a safe environment, in a manner that doesn't hurt anyone else and in a context of persons who can offer permission and respond with professional understanding.

For many of us, such a depth of emotional expression might not be necessary. However, it's important for each of us to find ways to express how we feel with one or more other persons who can show us genuine compassion and acceptance and who can respond in a competent and confidential manner. Do you concur?

(pause to reflect)

One of the most crucial ways I have learned to stop fearing others who have a different sexual orientation or gender identity will be examined in the next chapter of the book. As a theological framework for that chapter, as well as this one, let's keep in mind significant perspectives that are at the core of biblical understanding.

One perspective comes from the prophet Isaiah who speaks on behalf of God, and reminds us of an important reason to stop fearing others, "Do not fear, for I am with you; do not be afraid, for I am your God; I will strengthen you, I will help you, I will uphold you with my victorious right hand" (41:10).

A second perspective, one that offers a word of promise, comes from Jesus: "Peace I leave with you; my peace I give to you. I do not give to you as the world gives. Do not let your hearts be troubled, and do not let them be afraid" (John 14:27).

A third perspective, one that states rather categorically that there is no fear in love, comes from the writer of First John:

> God is love, and those who abide in love abide in God, and God abides in them. Love has been perfected among us in this: that we may have boldness on the day of judgment,

because as he is, so are we in this world. *There is no fear in love, but perfect love casts out fear;* for fear has to do with punishment, and whoever fears has not reached perfection in love. We love because he first loved us. Those who say, "I love God," and hate their brothers or sisters, are liars; for those who do not love a brother or sister whom they have seen, cannot love God whom they have not seen. The commandment we have from him is this: those who love God must love their brothers and sisters also (4:16-21).

These passages of Scripture provide the foundation for overcoming fear. But they will not make a difference unless we understand them, affirm them, and integrate them into our lives.

QUESTIONS

1. *When you think about persons who are LGBTQ, what thoughts come to mind?*

2. *When you get in touch with feelings you have toward persons who are LGBTQ, what emotions come to the surface?*

3. *Are you able to identify and name what might cause you to fear persons different from you? If so, are you also willing to do that right now?*

4. *Are you able to identify and name what might lead other persons different from you to fear you? If you are, are you willing to do that right now?*

5. *Do you know a person whose wisdom you respect, and whose spirit you can trust, with whom you can share your thoughts and feelings regarding your own fear? If so, would having a conversation with this person make sense? If you don't know such a person, would it be worthwhile to look for such a person?*

6. *On the basis of your own reflections and your interactions with others, is it time to stop fearing persons who have a sexual orientation or gender identity different from your own? What do you think?*

Is it time to stop socializing only with persons of our own sexual orientation or gender identity?

Maybe yes. Maybe no. What do you think?

I met him about a decade ago, when he was a student in an intensive seminary course I taught called "Loss and Grief." It was a seminar limited to fifteen students that met four hours a day, for two weeks.

Some of those who signed up for the class I had met before. But this student from another seminary I had not met until the first day of class. After introductions and a review of the syllabus, I indicated the assignment for the next day would be a three-page summary of personal experiences of loss. The first two pages would delineate important losses each student had undergone; the third page would be a description of the loss that was most significant, and the reasons why that loss was singled out.

I told the students that I would read them that afternoon, give them all an A grade, return them the next day, and never share anything with the class that they had written. The summaries would give me an awareness of what losses each class member had experienced before taking the course.

This particular student wrote that he was gay and had just broken up with the man whom he had believed would be his lifetime partner—an event that had happened only a few weeks before the course began and had led him to sign up for the course. He did not want and did not expect this breakup to occur. He was devastated!

I spoke with him the following day before class began and asked if he would like to talk with me after class—perhaps over lunch—and he readily agreed. That conversation began a series of meetings throughout the course. He became a mentor to me as I listened and learned—time and time again!

I began my teaching and administrative career thinking of myself as a mentor to students. I learned that it was more meaningful to practice mentoring as a mutual activity—student to professor, as well as professor to student. I also learned that in some situations—particularly when another person had experiences that were beyond my life situation (e.g., gender, race, sexual orientation, gender identity)—I needed students to mentor me.

My conversations with this particular student were primarily reverse mentoring. He helped me learn in a variety of ways. One example took place toward the end of the first week of class when we were beginning to discuss articles we had read regarding disenfranchised grief. He asked in class that morning if he could tell his story. I indicated he could—if that's what he wanted to do. For about twenty minutes he told how he had experienced disenfranchised grief when he and his partner had broken up. Students were deeply engaged as they listened to him, asked him questions, and shared some of their thoughts.

Learning from this student during that class was one of many such conversations I've had over the past forty years—from the time I taught the college course, "The Meaning of Sex," up to the present. During these years I've become convinced that the most important thing persons can do—if they really want to understand homosexuality (and all its related categories)—is to socialize with persons who have a sexual orientation or gender identity different from their own. Would you agree with such a perspective?

Is there any substitute for socializing? Is there an alternative that would work just as well? or an alternative that would work even better? I don't know, but I do know—personally—that socializing is effective for (1) getting to know others who have a sexual orientation or gender identity different from our own, (2) understanding what they are thinking, (3) sensing what they are feeling, (4) grasping what they are experiencing, and (5) becoming aware of what they are and are not seeking.

(pause to reflect)

This is what this student did for me and for the other students in our class. It's what others have also done for me—over and over again. Even while writing the final two chapters of this book, I've conversed with, and learned from, several individuals. One was a man I met at church. We had seen each other, but had never spoken. We introduced ourselves in a hallway one day, while we were each waiting to connect with different individuals. He had previously visited the church bookstore and looked at books I had written.

"Are you writing another book?" he asked.

"Yes, I am."

"On what topic?"

"It's a book about homosexuality."

He smiled and said, "That's me!"

I didn't know that about him, but it certainly opened the door to further conversation. When we decided to meet again, he asked if he could invite his husband to join us. I indicated that would be fine. We met, got acquainted, listened, and learned.

As a result of my asking social acquaintances during this last phase of my writing what they were doing that was interesting, and their asking me similar questions, I've ended up talking with a variety of individuals: two gay men, two lesbian women, a transgendered man, parents of a transgendered son, and a grandparent of a transgendered grandson, as well as a number of straight individuals. All of these contacts came about through casual conversations with people I know.

Recently an acquaintance asked me how he might meet "people who are homosexuals"—his words. I discussed a variety of options, realizing for him, and sometimes other heterosexual persons, making contact is not as easy as it might seem. If you're asking the same question, I would offer these suggestions: (1) think about whom you already know; (2) ask family members, social acquaintances, or people at church; (3) go to places that foster an open and inclusive atmosphere; or (4) simply let other people know your interest. One further possibility might be to pray and ask God to lead you to connect with persons you'd like to get to know.

To show proper respect for others, it's important to refrain from assuming everyone you meet is a heterosexual person. It's also important to refrain from asking others about their sexual orientation or gender identity. Let them tell you what they want you to know, as well as how and when they want to tell you. Persons are often willing to share after a relationship has been established—at least in a minimal manner. Also, keep in mind that sharing is a two-way street.

After you've met someone whose sexual orientation or gender identity is different from yours, and you would like to become better acquainted, you might consider saying: "I'd like to get to know you better." Or, "Would you be willing to meet for coffee or lunch?"

Or, "I'd like to learn from you." Or something else in your own words.

If your relationship with LGBTQ persons develops into an honest and candid exchange, be prepared to learn about experiences some persons have had that might include deep pain, profound hurt, and incredible anguish. When people have been judged and condemned many times for their sexual orientation or gender identity, it is natural to react with intense feelings. And let's not forget that some of that condemnation comes from pastors and laypeople in churches—some that are United Methodist. These persons—sometimes without fully realizing it—communicate rejection rather than acceptance—not only in words spoken (as negative as that might be) but also in feelings expressed (as powerful as those might be) and deeds carried out (as devastating as they sometimes are).

(pause to reflect)

If your conversation includes LGBTQ persons who believe they are called to ordained ministry within The United Methodist Church, be prepared to hear stories of individuals who are experiencing enormous conflict. They want to follow their calling, but oftentimes a staff-parish relations committee or a District Committee on Ministry or a Board of Ordained Ministry will not approve them, leaving them in an incredibly difficult place—called by God and, at the same time, rejected by persons who make decisions regarding their living out their calling. Listen carefully. Try to understand. Feel the anguish. Find ways to love.

It is my hope and prayer that anyone reading this book will be open to hearing stories of children, youth, and adults who have been hurt, and will feel their pain, as they describe their condemnation and rejection—perhaps by a father, a mother, a brother, a sister, a friend, a neighbor, a social acquaintance, a pastor, a church leader.

I've heard many stories from LGBTQ persons, have tried to carefully listen to them, have felt their anguish as deeply as I could, and have grieved with them. I've also had conversations with other LGBTQ persons who are not living with the hurt I have described and have not experienced it personally. However, most of them are keenly aware of others who have been deeply hurt.

Hopefully the day will come when attitudes and actions of all persons—at least within The United Methodist Church—will accept, affirm, and genuinely love all persons, regardless of sexual orientations and gender identities!

In the previous chapter we explored whether the time had come to stop fearing persons who have a sexual orientation or gender identity different from our own. Toward the end of that discussion I indicated I would identify an overall thesis in this chapter that would speak to that question. Here's what my experience has taught me: *Socializing—at a deep and profound level—with others who have a sexual orientation or gender identity different from our own is one of the most important ways to overcome fear.*

I really believe this! Do you?

(pause to reflect)

Two things have impressed me in my relationships with persons who have a sexual orientation or gender identity different from mine—in recent years as well as throughout my lifetime. One is *how often and how much we are the same.* Our primary values, our basic beliefs, our daily activities, our hopes and dreams—even our relationships—have dimensions that are the same.

For example, a relationship of trust between a man and a woman is the same as a relationship of trust between two women or two men. Intimacy between a man and a woman is the same as the intimacy between two women or two men. A monogamous relationship between a man and a woman is the same as a monogamous relationship between two women or two men.

A second impression is *how relatively little sex has to do with homosexuality in a monogamous relationship.* Two lesbian women, or two gay men, live together and carry on their lives in a manner that, in many ways, is the same as a straight couple: get up in the morning, take showers, eat breakfast, go to work outside the home (or in the home), care for the children (if there are any), go to the grocery store on the way home, stop for gas, arrive home, get the mail, make dinner (if it's your turn), and on and on. Whatever the household, whatever the sexual orientation, so much of it is the same!

Perhaps a focus on the ways we are the same, together with the important but limited role of sex in our lives, could make a significant contribution to our conversation. Perhaps such an approach could also lead us toward becoming the persons God is calling us to be!

QUESTIONS

1. *How would you describe sexual diversity in the world in which you live—family, friends, church members (if you're part of a church), and social acquaintances?*

2. *If you are straight, have you become acquainted with LGBTQ persons? If so, what have you learned about them? What have they learned about you?*

3. *If you are part of a local congregation that is predominantly straight, do you think it would be a helpful learning experience to have LGBTQ persons join you and others in an educational setting? If so, whom might you invite?*

4. *If you are straight, have you listened to stories by LGBTQ persons who have experienced condemnation and rejection? If so, in what ways did they help you understand their experiences?*

5. *Do you agree that socializing is one of the most important activities for overcoming fear of others? If so, what do you mean when you say that you agree?*

6. *On the basis of your own reflections and your interactions with others, is it time to stop socializing only with persons of your own sexual orientation or gender identity? What do you think?*

Is it time to start expending our full energy on the mission of The United Methodist Church: *to make disciples of Jesus Christ for the transformation of the world?*

Maybe yes. Maybe no. What do you think?

Of the many questions that this book asks, perhaps there's one that makes many of us feel most uncomfortable. Whether you lean to the left socially and theologically, or to the right, or you are somewhere in between, it is clear that The United Methodist Church is painfully distracted from its stated mission by the ongoing debates, rancor, and divisions about the issue of homosexuality.

Have we become guilty of idolatry—raising the issue of sexuality to a level that exceeds its value in comparison to our call to be focused on the gospel? There certainly are many important issues involved in the current debates over homosexuality, but do any of them rise to the level of replacing the gospel?

We might ask: What does God want us to learn from this debate over homosexuality? Surely God wants us to learn more than which side of the debate is correct, or which side should be declared the winner. If this debate is more than just a contest, what does God want us to learn?

(pause to reflect)

Are some people using the current debate about homosexuality as a way of avoiding the issues of unfaithfulness within the heterosexual community? Are some enjoying the drama of this debate, because it allows them to avoid pursuing our mission of making disciples? Are some of the advocacy groups—on various sides of this issue—raising money and gaining power by fomenting division within the church? Are some of us in The United Methodist Church so used to being sick with decline and division that we are unwilling to take steps to become well as a church?

(pause to reflect)

Is it possible that the lesson of the current divisions over homosexuality is the lesson of priority and perspective? Does God want us to see that nothing—not even important debates about this issue—should displace our call to be focused on *making disciples of Jesus Christ for the transformation of the world*?

(pause to reflect)

Is it time to leave room for disagreements on matters that are important but do not rise to the level of replacing the gospel? Is it time to learn to live with tensions that are not entirely resolved?

Is it time to stop using excessive amounts of energy—time,

money, and engagement—dealing with the subject of homosexuality? Is it time to stop speaking words and carrying out actions that are biased, intolerant, mean, injurious—even at times vicious and hateful?

Is it time—on a personal level—to repent of making an important matter the most important one and treating one another in unloving ways? and then to seek forgiveness and offer forgiveness to others within and beyond the UMC?

Is it time—on an organizational level (Good News Movement, Reconciling Churches Network, Confessing Movement, Love Prevails, Wesleyan Covenant Association, Methodist Federation for Social Action, and others)—to repent of making an important matter the most important one and treating one another in unloving ways? and then to seek forgiveness and offer forgiveness to others within and beyond the UMC?

What do you think?

Resources

Utilizing online resources is essential. They are plentiful—almost inexhaustible—yet they are not always dependable sources of accurate information. The websites I am listing are, from my perspective, reliable sources of information, even though you may not agree with some of the points of view set forth.

American Medical Association	ama-assn.org
American Psychological Association	apa.org
Confessing Movement	confessingumc.org
Gay Christian Network	gaychristian.net
Good News Movement	goodnewsmag.org
Judicial Council	umc.org/decisions/search
Love Prevails	loveprevailsumc.com
Methodist Federation for Social Action	mfsaweb.org
National Association of Social Workers	naswdc.org
Planned Parenthood	plannedparenthood.org
Reconciling Ministries Network	rmnetwork.org
The United Methodist Church	umc.org
Wesleyan Covenant Association	wesleyancovenant.org

CPSIA information can be obtained
at www.ICGtesting.com
Printed in the USA
LVOW03s2221061017
551513LV00007B/10/P